THE WAR
ILLUSTRATORS

D1257142

FRONTISPIECE
Caricature of William Simpson sketching on the battlefield
The Bailie, Vol V No 118, Glasgow, 1874
(Victoria and Albert Museum)

THE WAR ILLUSTRATORS

Compiled and written by

PAT HODGSON

MACMILLAN PUBLISHING CO., INC.
New York

Copyright © 1977 Pat Hodgson

All rights reserved. No part of this book may be reproduced or
transmitted in any form or by any means, electronic or
mechanical, including photocopying, recording or by any
information storage and retrieval system, without permission in
writing from the Publisher.

Macmillan Publishing Co., Inc.
866 Third Avenue, New York, N.Y. 10022

Library of Congress Cataloging in Publication Data
Hodgson, Pat.
    The war illustrators.
    1. War in art.   2. Magazine illustration—
Great Britain.   3. Magazine illustration—United
States.   4. War correspondents—Great Britain.
5. War correspondents—United States.   I.   Title.
NC968.5.W35H6   741.65   76-47458
ISBN 0-02-552000-8

Designed by Behram Kapadia

Photography by John R. Freeman, Sally Chappell, Leo Siegel,
and the National Army Museum, London

First American Edition 1977

Printed in Great Britain

741.65
H691w
C-1
12.95
10/79

Contents

CAMBRIA COUNTY LIBRARY
JOHNSTOWN, PA. 15901

Alfred R. Waud (1828–91)

William Waud (d. 1878)

Edwin Forbes (1839–95)

Henry Lovie

Melton Prior (1845-1910)

Anon

Johann Nepomuk Schönberg (1844-?)

Walter Paget

Frank Algernon Stewart (1877-?)

Howard Chandler Christy (1873-1952)

Ernest Prater

Inglis Sheldon-Williams (1870-1940)

Anon

Introduction

Pictorial journalism effectively commenced with the foundation of the *Illustrated London News* in 1842. Technically the time was right for its inception as it was now possible for wood blocks of pictures to be printed alongside type for long runs. The climate of opinion at the time was also favourable, as illustrated papers had an instant appeal for a new public that had only just learnt to read and was eager for information. As Mason Jackson, an early art editor of the *Illustrated London News* said, picture papers are 'to a certain extent, independent of language; they are prized alike by the civilized foreigner and the untutored savage.'[1] In England their progress was intimately connected with the wars of the Empire, which provided escapist adventure stories for the stay-at-home public for the last fifty years of the nineteenth century. There was sometimes unexpected proof of the wide appeal of picture papers. When the British were self-righteously sacking the palace of the 'untutored savage' Ashanti king at Coomassie in 1874, they found copies of the *Illustrated London News* in the royal library. War correspondence was itself a new art. Before the Crimean War most newspaper accounts of warfare were based on bulletins issued by the generals. The campaign in the Crimea saw the first true war correspondents in the modern meaning of the term, who, with the artists, brought their own personal comment to the scene and interpreted events in a more understandable way through a skilful combination of entertainment and information.

There have always been war artists who have painted a picture to commemorate a battle or to show the glories or miseries of war. A war illustrator working for the pictorial press had a different function. He was as much a journalist as an artist and his job was to depict current news as quickly as possible, by means of a rapid sketch and written report, and let the engraver at home redraw his work on to a block with suitable embellishments for publication. Until photographic methods were generally used to place the drawing on a block in the 1880s, the engraver had complete control over the finished reproduction. This naturally led to bad feeling between artist and engraver, and Rossetti spoke for all artists when he wrote:

O Woodman spare that block—
O gash not anyhow!
It took ten days by clock—
I'd fain protect it now!

An engraver worked slowly and a full-page *Illustrated London News* picture might take one man three weeks to complete. A speedier method was devised in 1860 by Charles Wells. Several pieces of boxwood were bolted together to make a block of the required size. A thin coating of white paint was spread over the surface to get a good background for the drawing which was then sketched on. Next the block was separated into its component parts and distributed among several engravers. Each engraver had a subject he was good at, and worked on that part of the block. One did skies, another trees, another faces, and so on. It was very much a routine job, and most of the original vigour of the sketch was lost. Sometimes the blocks were inaccurately bolted back into position for printing, and the dividing lines could be clearly seen on the finished reproduction. It was small wonder that artists were dissatisfied with the result. Where the original sketches survive they have an impact and freshness which is invariably missing from the engraved reproduction. A Victorian blandness seemed to overcome the engravers, who completely obliterated the feeling of immediacy inherent in a sketch hurriedly completed at the front. Unfortunately most of the early sketches for British journals have been lost, so the skill of some of these artists has to be guessed at. From the few originals that are still in existence, the majority from American journals, the liveliness and vitality of the illustrators' work can still be appreciated.

The *Illustrated London News*, founded by Herbert Ingram, was the first journal to present news and pictures together as a regular policy. The paper was published weekly, cost 6d, and the first issue contained 16 printed pages and 32 woodcuts. Disasters, murders and wars always make popular reading, and the *Illustrated London News*'s sales were more than doubled by the revolutionary wars of 1848. The Crimean War, which was the first major conflict since Waterloo and took place in an exotic land, was an obvious place to send some of the new 'special artists' in 1854. The war was a journalistic landmark in other ways as it marked the beginning of war photography, although the photographers, notably Roger Fenton and James Robertson, went out privately and not under the auspices of a newspaper. Although the discovery of photography was contemporary with the founding of the illustrated press, actual photographs were not reproduced until the 1890s, when a satisfactory method of printing half-tones was discovered. Up to that time a photograph had to be converted into a line drawing for reproduction. Engravings based on photographs can usually be distinguished from those originating from sketches as there is no sign of action in the former, the people look stiff and the perspective distorted.

War correspondence was also taking on a new form in the Crimea, led by William Howard Russell of *The Times*. His critical approach alarmed the British generals, who were not used to this kind of thing. Increasingly it became the practice for the same man to double as correspondent, artist and perhaps photographer when working for the illustrated press. Throughout the century news and sketches were also sometimes provided by combatants. It often took so long to get a correspondent out to a war that all action might be over before he arrived, and so serving officers were commissioned by the papers to send back material, at any rate until the professional 'special' turned up. Some of these soldiers, like George Atkinson and Henry Hope Crealock, were talented artists in their own right, and others merely supplied rough sketches which could be redrawn at the London office. The practice was still being followed in 1897 when *The Regiment* reported that the London District of the Institute of Journalists had protested about the number of officers being used as correspondents at the Boer War. The writer indignantly held that combatants were best adapted to write about a war, and if they were the sole correspondents 'in all probability less "bosh" would continue to appear in the daily papers' (9 January 1897).

Somewhere between the Academy war artist and the 'special' of the illustrated journals, was the artist sent out to the front by a publisher to provide paintings which could be reproduced as lithographic prints. This method of making prints was particularly popular in the 1850s and 60s. The prints had no current news value, but were based on personal observation and provided a colourful souvenir of the war. They were usually published in sets with very detailed captions. Day & Son were at this time leading lithographic printers in England, and Currier & Ives held the same position in America.

William Simpson, familiarly known to the public as 'Crimean Simpson', first specialized in this kind of picture, and published two volumes of lithographs on the Crimea entitled *The Seat of the War in the East*. Simpson was sent to the Crimea by the London print seller, Colnaghi, and arrived there in November 1854 with letters of introduction to some of the officers. As a correspondent or artist had to provide his own transport and food in the early days, it was always advisable to have friends in high places, or else to possess a gregarious disposition and the ability to wheedle quarters and food from the officers. From the start Simpson made a point of keeping on the right side of authority. He always cleared his drawings with Lord Raglan, and when they reached England, by way of Lord Raglan's letter-bag, they were scrutinized by the Duke of Newcastle as War Minister, and finally by Queen Victoria. In his autobiography Simpson said that although he found a 'Special Correspondent' was regarded with more respect than a 'Special Artist', everyone at the front was much more friendly towards the artist, as he was less critical. Lord Raglan's staff were probably still smarting from the highly critical reports that Russell was sending back to *The Times*. On his return to England Simpson was able to spend some time working up the sketches he had made at the front, and to sell them individually. This was a recognized source of income for 'specials' who could often live for some years on the proceeds from the exhibition of their war sketches and from formal paintings based on the original drawings. The *Sphere* referred to this fifty years later when it described war artists returning from the Boer War, 'bringing with them a great many sketches which will probably bear fruit as thrilling pictures in oils at the galleries in the autumn' (4 August 1900).

The *Illustrated London News* was unchallenged in England until 1869. In the early years the war illustrators were not always credited, but by the end of the Crimean War four artists of note had emerged. These were Joseph A. Crowe, Edward A. Goodall, Robert T. Landells and William Simpson. Crowe and Goodall were essentially good watercolourists who vanished from the scene as war artists after the Crimea, although Crowe continued for some years as a correspondent before taking up a diplomatic career. Landells became a specialist in Prussian affairs and continued to work as a war illustrator until the Franco-Prussian War of 1870–1. Frank Vizetelly was another accomplished *Illustrated London News* 'special' of the early period. He recorded the march of Garibaldi and his red-shirts in 1860–1, went on to the American Civil War, the War of 1866 and the Carlist insurrection of 1868 before losing his life in Egypt with Hicks Pasha in 1883.

In 1869 the *Graphic*, a new illustrated weekly, was founded by William Luson Thomas in time to send a team of artists to the

Franco-Prussian War. Thomas made it his policy to welcome to the staff any artist of talent, regardless of what medium he normally used, rather than confine the copying of sketches to a special staff of draughtsmen on wood. An exhibition of war sketches from both journals opened at the Crystal Palace in October 1870. The catalogue says: 'They have a far higher interest than many more finished productions, as they were taken on the spot, at the risk of life and limb.' 'We may also say that this country has every reason to be proud of the two journals we have named for in few things can England boast a more decided superiority than in illustrated papers. America is far behind in this respect.' The catalogue makes another interesting comment on the nature of the war illustrator's work at this time: 'A survey of these sketches convinces us that a newspaper with good engravers and inferior artists will turn out better and more faithful pictures than one whose artists are excellent, but whose engravers can only copy what is before them. The engraver who works from field drawings must complete them as he goes.' The engraver did not always in fact copy the sketch on to the wood block, but another artist might be used for the job. Sydney P. Hall did his first work for the *Graphic* at the Franco-Prussian War, and the exhibition catalogue notes that his 'drawings are good, but he gives a great deal of work to the engraver.' Hall became a regular artist for the *Graphic* but did not work as an illustrator at the front again.

Meanwhile in Europe and America the progress of pictorial journalism followed much the same lines as in Britain. A year after the *Illustrated London News* was founded, *L'Illustration* commenced publication in Paris and *Illustrierte Zeitung* in Leipzig. Other illustrated papers of the period in Europe included *Le Monde Illustré* and *Univers Illustré* in France, and *Ueber Land und Meer* published in Stuttgart. The first Russian picture paper was *Russkii Khudozhestvennyi*, established in 1851. On 16 December 1855 Frank Leslie, a wood engraver who had worked for the *Illustrated London News*, founded *Frank Leslie's Illustrated Newspaper* in America. He ambitiously recorded: 'Our journal is the most comprehensive and interesting pictorial record of events to be found in either hemisphere' (Vol. I, 1855). Two years later another picture paper, *Harper's Weekly*, was inaugurated by Fletcher Harper.

The American Civil War was one of the best visually recorded wars of the nineteenth century. Apart from the magnificent photographs taken by Matthew Brady and his colleagues, many artists enlisted in the armies and *Leslie's* and *Harper's* had their own 'specials'. Edwin Forbes, who worked for *Leslie's*, lived for the rest of his life on sketches made during the war. He worked them up as paintings or etchings, later publishing two volumes of etchings on the subject, *Life Studies of the Great Army* (1876) and *Thirty Years After* (1891). Henri Lovie also drew for *Leslie's* and a few months before the end of the war the journal boasted that during the past four years at least one of its 'trained corps of the first artists' had been at every important expedition, and that three thousand pictures of 'battles, sieges, bombardments, stormings and other scenes, incidental to war' had been published, contributed by more than 80 artists (Vol. XIX, p. 146, 26 November 1864). *Harper's* had the Waud brothers, who had come over from London in 1858, Thomas Nast, the cartoonist, Winslow Homer and Theodore R. Davis as accredited artists.

The *Cincinnati Times* felt that many of the battle scenes in the illustrated journals were 'little better than a sensational farce' (2 July 1862). It later quotes an instance when army trains near Chattanooga were set on fire in October 1863, and there were some 'on the spot' drawings, although the artist was known to have been in bed asleep when the incident occurred. On the same theme, a cartoon appeared in *Vanity Fair* showing 'Our Own Artist' using toy soldiers for models when sketching General Banks's army in action (14 September 1861).

The Federal side was the best recorded, but many of the most interesting pictures of the Confederates came from the English journalist Frank Vizetelly working for the *Illustrated London News*. Some of his drawings when lost in transit were pirated by *Harper's*. Vizetelly was a convivial character, and Major Heros von Borcke of the Prussian army, who served with the Confederate General Stuart, has left this description of him: 'He was not long in becoming a general favourite at headquarters. Regularly after dinner, our whole family of officers, from the commander down to the youngest lieutenant, used to assemble in his tent, squeezing ourselves into narrow quarters to hear his entertaining narratives.' Generally speaking the American illustrated journals were not much interested in the little wars of British imperialism which recurred throughout the latter part of the nineteenth century and, if illustrating them, would use a picture made by one of the British artists on the spot and simultaneously published in a British journal.

The Siege of Paris, 1870–1, was a high spot for war correspondents and artists and made exciting copy for the readers of illustrated journals. Some artists, like Jules Pelcoq who worked for the *Illustrated London News*, were confined in the city and had their sketches sent off by balloon to London. The drawings were usually photographed and copies sent off by a number of different balloons so that there was a fair chance of one of them reaching its destination. Pelcoq, a Parisian, suffered severely from cold during the siege as there was no fuel to warm his apartment, and was often forced to complete his sketches in bed, muffled up in a blanket.

Other Frenchmen also acted as artists and correspondents for the British journals, including M. Moullin for the *Illustrated London News* and M. Mejanel for the *Graphic*. Their work is not always credited, so it is difficult to determine whether they actually provided sketches or just a detailed bulletin. However, the *Graphic* refers to Mejanel's presence at the bombardment of Sedan, saying: 'The sketch is from M. Mejanel's pencil, who was in the thick of the bloody business. Remaining on the high ground, as long as it was safe to stay, he was able to perceive clearly how the Prussians were gradually converging on the fated stronghold.'

Sydney Hall of the *Graphic* was one of the artists reporting from outside Paris with the Prussian army. When he managed to get into the city, on 6 February 1871, he visited the bureau of the French journal *L'Illustration* and commented: 'The editor in a gorgeous uniform – I don't know that he wasn't a general, and the sub-editor a colonel.' While he was in Paris he dined with the correspondents of *The Times, Standard* and *Daily Telegraph* who had been there throughout the siege.

The French pictorial press of the time does not always clearly credit its illustrators, but the French artists Daumier, Manet, Robida, Vierge and Cham have all left striking records of Paris under siege. The *Graphic* believed that the war artist had come of age at the Franco-Prussian War. 'The artist has manifested himself as necessary now to the due reporting of important occurrences as the special correspondent.' 'We have been enabled week by week to set before the public a pictorial chronicle of the war even to its minor incidents. And our art has not been tinctured by the old fashioned classicality which indulged in many fanciful flights, departed from truth wherever such a step was deemed convenient, and shrunk from accuracy wherever a feature presented itself of a character that might be thought too homely or uncomely' (18 February 1871).

It is possible to get some idea of how the early illustrators worked from a handful of sketches which have survived. Frank Leslie provided a special sketchbook for his artists to use, complete with copyright notice on the bottom left-hand corner, and Henri Lovie's drawings have numerous instructions written over them to guide the engravers. Artists employed a kind of pictorial shorthand, using a combination of drawing and words to get their message across, leaving their colleagues at home to make the sketch into a picture. They were not idle in camp and employed themselves in making detailed drawings of uniforms, gun carriages, horses and other military paraphernalia which could be used for reference. The home-based artists must also have had many reference books, prints and photographs to help them to get the detail right if the 'special' had not been very explicit.

Mason Jackson, in *The Pictorial Press: Its Origins and Progress*, gives an example of the way in which an original sketch might be transformed. The artist's impression of the surrender of Sedan shows evidence of being drawn in a hurry, under fire. When the picture was published in the *Illustrated London News* on 17 September 1870 only a small portion of the drawing was used. 'The cream or heart of the sketch, representing an officer waving a white flag over the gate of Sedan attended by a trumpeter, was taken for the subject, while the comparatively unimportant part of the sketch was left out.'

The correspondent's first duty was to make efficient arrangements to get a report back to his editor. Simpson always said that his first job was to find the post office and to post all the packets himself, having once had all his work lost when he entrusted it to *The Times* correspondent for posting. There was a time-lag between the sending of a despatch and its arrival at home. Material coming from the Crimea was delayed about three weeks, and from China and India it was likely to take months. Often news was received of an important battle or the fall of a fort weeks before a written report or sketch arrived from the correspondent. This did not seem to matter to the public too much, and the pictures when they finally did come were used for several succeeding issues, and sometimes for the Christmas number as well.

In his autobiography Simpson describes a scoop when he was present at the fall of Strasbourg during the Franco-Prussian War. He completed his drawing in the early hours of the morning after the fighting and walked five miles to General Werder's headquarters so that the sketch could be despatched. 'I was up with the first streak of light, and did a sketch of the event of the day before. This I had to take to Mundalsheim to the post. I calculated that if sent off that day it would reach Mr

Jackson, the editor, in time for "next Saturday", which it did.'

The last thirty years of the nineteenth century were the golden years for war illustrators. Never again were they to have such influence and fame. The flowering of the art was essentially a British phenomenon, and was dependent on the traditions of imperialism, the army and a moral conviction that native races should accept British government for their own good. As Archibald Forbes said of the British victory over the Zulus, in *Memories and Studies of War and Peace* (1895), 'It did one good to see the glorious old "white arm" reassert again its pristine prestige.' The actions that were fought in the cause of Empire were in exotic surroundings, and usually involved only a small number of troops. As it took so long for the correspondent to get to the battle zone, all his preliminary reports dealt with his adventures on the journey and understandably he built himself into the hero of an exciting story. People followed his reports and drawings eagerly week by week, and the correspondent began to live up to the image.

War illustrators and reporters became the *élite* of the journalistic profession, and developed a swashbuckling Hemingway-like group personality which they presented to the public. They maintained their own legend, referring to each other in despatches and drawings. They messed together, had close friends among the other correspondents, and by the 1880s formed an influential press corps which looked after its own. It was essentially a close-knit London group, but although many gave generous help to each other, some had less worthy reasons for keeping together. In *Villiers: His Five Decades of Adventure*, Frederic Villiers said: 'Birds of this feather generally flock together, not out of affection for each other's society, but to keep watch on one another and to jump the news if possible.' The 'specials' had to be able to turn a hand to anything, to be expert horsemen, take part in the fighting, help with the wounded and somehow get their despatches home to their journals.

They behaved with impressive coolness under fire. ' "Hallo, Prior, you had a close shave that time," said Stanley, as he rose and took a big slug out of the wall within two inches of where my head had been,' writes Melton Prior in *Campaigns of a War Correspondent*. He was a war illustrator in over twenty-four campaigns for the *Illustrated London News*. Similar sang-froid was shown by Frederic Villiers at his first campaign for the *Graphic* in Serbia in 1876. As the bullets whistled past on Mount Yavor he mused, 'Should I ever return to my dear mother?', and after the battle had raged round him for some time decided: 'By Jove, it's high time to go.'[2] In his autobiography William Simpson boasts of actually taking a barricade from the Communards in Paris in 1871. 'I have always claimed that I took that barricade, because I was the first man in it. Of course I was heavily armed with a sketch book, a pencil, and a penknife.' It was not always easy to sketch under battle conditions and Prior described, again in *Campaigns of a War Correspondent*, how, at Tel-el-Magfar in 1882, he 'lay flat on the ground with my sketch book in front of me, and set to work while the two guns on either side were pounding away for all they were worth.' An Egyptian shell landed near and covered him with sand, but 'never mind, I have got a jolly good sketch.'

In spite of these mock heroics, war correspondence could be a dangerous job. There is a memorial in St Paul's Cathedral to the seven newspapermen who did not return from the Sudan campaign. Only one of these was an illustrator, Frank Vizetelly, and the others included John Cameron of the *Standard* and St Leger Herbert of the *Morning Post*, both well-known figures in the press camp. There was always danger from disease in a tropical climate. G. W. Steevens of the *Daily Mail* died of enteric fever during the siege of Ladysmith at the age of thirty, and his great friend, the *Daily Graphic* artist W. T. Maud, who had devotedly nursed him, died only three years later, probably as a consequence of the same fever.

Correspondents were always complaining about the problems for an artist in an inhospitable climate. Dr Doyle Glanville, who provided many sketches of the Zulu War for the *Illustrated London News*, drew a picture of himself on the job 'with the thermometer registering 96 or 100 degrees in the shade, and surrounded by a group of odiferous natives, all talking and gesticulating about the picture. Nearly eaten up by countless flies',[3] he considered that art in Africa was no easy pastime. The Khartoum relief column provided some comic diversion of a perilous kind as almost every correspondent fell in the Nile at some time or another. Prior and Villiers both provided lively drawings of the incidents, and *Black and White* published a drawing covered with splodges saying that 'the red waters of the Nile – not Mr Sheldon – are responsible for these' (17 October 1896).

A war artist was also in more danger than other correspondents of being mistaken for a spy. In *The Pictorial Press: Its Origin and Progress*, Mason Jackson quotes from a letter by a war artist at the Franco-Prussian War, probably William Simpson, saying that he made his drawings on tissue paper, rolled them up as pills and placed them 'handy in my waistcoat pocket to be chewed up or swallowed if "in extremis" '. Simpson was in trouble at Metz where he found that 'the townspeople of Metz became quite wild when they heard of the French defeats at Wörth and Forbach, and when they saw an artist sketching the Emperor's carriage, they pounced upon him as a Prussian spy, and he and his companions were marched off into custody, amid the hootings of the mob.'[4] Jackson mentions another artist who found himself under close observation by the police at Bremerhafen, so he nonchalantly sketched out a drawing with his umbrella on the sand of the harbour, 'as if in a fit of abstraction', and memorized the sketch sufficiently to be able to commit it to paper at the railway station, far from the scene of the crime. Villiers found the Russians so suspicious of his motives when sketching at Kircheneff that 'I had to fall back on my thumb-nails and shirt cuffs instead of a notebook.'

It was understandable that combatants often suspected correspondents of being spies, especially when the pressmen went over to see how the opposing side was getting on. Frank Vizetelly, first with the Federal army in the American Civil War, for reasons of conscience transferred to the Confederates after his experiences in the captured city of Memphis. Villiers was with the Serbs in their fight against Turkey from 1875 to 1876, but changed to the Turkish side the following year when Russia joined in.

Everyone encountered censorship problems, on some occasions with their own military commanders and on others from suspicious foreigners. On the British side Sir Garnet Wolseley was particularly averse to correspondents, whom he referred to as 'a race of drones'. He kept them away from the front line, and was not above giving out false information. The French were inclined to give way to panic over spies and created some ugly situations for correspondents, while the Turks and Russians were always extremely suspicious and especially sensitive about criticism. When Melton Prior, as a 'special' at the Russo-Turkish War, found that his despatches were not getting through, he was forced to use blackmail. He told the Turkish commander that unless his sketches were passed he would return home and publish as many drawings as he could of Turkish atrocities to the Bulgarians. This seemed to work. The illustrated journals usually had 'specials' with both sides in any European war, although sometimes, for reasons of economy, they commissioned nationals of one of the countries concerned to send in sketches.

The most important figure of the great age of war illustrators was Melton Prior. He was first commissioned by William Ingram of the *Illustrated London News* in 1873 to go to the Ashanti War, and from then on was always ready to leave England at a moment's notice for foreign parts. He recalls, in *Campaigns of a War Correspondent*, how he was quickly plunged into the thick of the fighting. 'I may here mention that the correspondents were all armed with guns or rifles. I had a double-barrelled gun with swan-shot cartridges, and when the enemy at one time made an ugly rush in our direction we all let fly at them.' Sometimes he found the going hard, and when approaching Coomassie he was almost too tired to march into the town. He grabbed the tail of a mule in front of him to give himself some impetus. The mule turned out to belong to Sir Garnet Wolseley himself, who said kindly: 'Never mind, Prior, hold on, and we two will drag you in.'

After the Ashanti War Prior was sent to join the insurgent chief Peco Pavlovitch fighting the Turks in Herzegovina in 1875. He found Pavlovitch's martial ardour sometimes more than he could stomach. After a fearful battle with the Turks he noticed 'three curious mounds which reminded me of the way in which I had seen cannon-balls stacked at Woolwich. I asked what it was, and Peco, swinging his foot round, kicked the corner cannon-ball out, and to my horror I found it was a Turk's head.' In the war of 1877 he was sent to the Turkish side, and in 1878 covered the Kaffir War and followed this by service in the Zulu War of 1879–80, where he was one of the first to find the body of the Prince Imperial.

After some near misses from Zulu assegais, Prior returned home only to be sent out to South Africa for the 1st Boer War. It is interesting to learn that he reconstructed an illustration of the Majuba Hill action purely from a verbal report given to him by his friend, correspondent of the *Standard*, John Cameron. 1882 saw him in Egypt for the bombing of Alexandria and the battles of Tel-el-Kebir, El Teb and Tamai. He was with the Gordon Relief Expedition, where he had several narrow escapes. Various minor skirmishes took up his time for the next few years and in 1899 he went to the 2nd Boer War where he was confined in the siege of Ladysmith with several other correspondents. His last expedition for the *Illustrated London News* was to the Russo-Japanese War of 1904–5.

Prior was a likeable man who could write lively prose as well as being an accomplished artist. In South Africa in 1881 he described how his tent 'in the daytime was looked upon as an artist's studio, and became the rendezvous of all the best fellows in the camp during the lazy hours.' His servant concocted for them an Indian corn porridge which the men ate with condensed milk or jam. His friend Harry Furniss said of him, in *My Bohemian Days*, that he was 'an energetic, business-like artist, with tremendous vitality and a terribly shrill laugh.' He had a large head, was quite bald, and was known as 'the screeching billiard ball'. He was popular, clumsy, tactless and, as *The Times* said in his obituary, 'never lost a certain roughness of metaphor in his speech' (3 November 1910). He was conscientious and able, took part in the fighting, helped with the wounded, did the cooking when necessary and at all times was a completely dedicated correspondent.

Frederic Villiers was a similar legendary character, who saw more than forty years service as a war artist. He was first commissioned by the *Graphic* to go to Serbia in 1876 and his career followed a similar pattern to that of Prior's. He did not remain committed to one journal like Prior, however, but worked for all the leading illustrated papers, and later for a press agency and as a free-lance. He does not emerge as a very sympathetic character from his memoirs, although he had the usual number of hair-raising escapes. At the Battle of Tamai in 1884 he and the *Daily Telegraph* correspondent Bennet Burleigh were in the British square when it was broken by a 'howling mob of fanatics'. He could hear Burleigh shouting encouragement: 'Give it them! Hurrah! Three cheers – hurrah!', which helped to rally the soldiers and the enemy were beaten off. Villiers said: 'Regulation revolvers are not much use against fuzzy-wuzzy; he seems to swallow the bullets and come up smiling like the proverbial conjuror.'

Although undoubtedly brave, Villiers was a terrible *poseur* and did much to perpetuate his own legend. It is difficult to estimate his ability as an artist as little of his original work has survived. *The Times* was rather scathing about his skill, saying that although 'only an artist of moderate ability, he was able to combine both artistic and descriptive journalism, and in energy and perseverance made up for his lack of talents.' However, 'he always carried with him into the lecture room that air of the swashbuckler which was at one time comportment for the soldiers of the pen' (6 April 1922). In *Famous War Correspondents* F. Lauriston Bullard offers a possible solution as to why most of his sketches have been lost: 'With an army in the field he will keep industriously at work making sketches, but the close observer might alone detect his occupation, for his methods are quite his own. Much of the time he makes his drawings in tiny sketch books, so small that he may hold them in the palm of his hand.' Rudyard Kipling is supposed to have based the character of one of the war artists in *The Light that Failed* on Villiers, and Forbes Robertson came to him for advice when playing the part on the stage.

Villiers's personality was distinctly theatrical, and he took delight in lecturing on the wars in full campaign kit with medals, although in fairness it must be said that he was not the only one to do this. Harry Furniss, who had met most of the correspondents, described, in *My Bohemian Days*, how they 'spend money like princes and return as heroes; they appear on lecture platforms in their war-paint or in evening dress 'à la Forbes', their coats ablaze with foreign orders, or hanging from ribbons round their necks.'

In an extraordinary interview given to *Black and White* (19 January 1895) Villiers bears an uncanny resemblance to Evelyn Waugh's Apthorpe in *Men at Arms*. Of all the correspondents he was the most attached to his gear. The interviewer found the artist in the midst of 'a general chaos of trunks, sketch-books, and campaigning kit', making ready to leave for the Sino–Japanese War. Villiers said: 'This campaign will probably run into the winter months, and winter in Korea is no laughing matter. I am obliged to take heavy coats, furs and warm clothing generally, as well as some necessary gear for summer wear.' On campaign he would wear his wash leather vest, 'perforated in many places for ventilation', and special shooting breeches, because 'in a hot country where there is much sun, they keep the knee comparatively cool, and in the winter, as the blood can freely circulate, they are also warm.' Boots made of porpoise-hide were essential as they could also be slept in if the occasion demanded. In addition a water bottle and a revolver must be stowed into his Wolseley valise and a Burroughs and Wellcome medicine chest. His calculations did not include the possibility that a campaign might be unsuccessful, as he also carried evening clothes for the celebratory dinners which would be held afterwards. For his work he took paper, carbon and lead pencils, brushes and black and white paint. His sketches were small, and would be sent back in a special red priority envelope which had been invented by William Russell for the press during the Crimean War. He always carried a Kodak No. 3 Junior hand camera. Considering that on occasion he had also been known to arrive on campaign complete with ciné camera and a bicycle, and had invented a tent built on the principle of a 'glorified umbrella', he must have been a formidable sight when he turned up at the front. Villiers continued as a 'special' until 1914 when he joined the French army and fought in the First World War.

Improvements in printing towards the end of the century completely altered the presentation of a war artist's work. The use of photography meant that an original sketch could be reproduced, and from about 1882 pictures appear in the *Illustrated London News* labelled 'facsimile of sketch'. The development of a half-tone process not only meant that photographs could now be reproduced in the journals, but also that wash drawings and paintings could be printed. The Christmas Number of the *Graphic*, 1889, described for its readers some of the new printing processes. 'In quiet times fifty-five engravers are necessary to produce the weekly *Graphic*, but at busy periods the number is greatly increased.' The reproduction of full-page engravings might cost 50 guineas. The drawings for process engraving were generally pen and ink on smooth paper or cardboard. They were reduced by photography to the correct size, 'printed on sensitized zinc, and then bitten out by acid. A second process is often added, producing a tone or tint, by the aid of small dots or points, the artist marking on his drawings the part he wishes so treated.' 'A quicker process is to omit photography and make the drawing direct on transfer paper. It is then transferred to stone by a lithographic press, and then on to the zinc plate.'

Pictures could now be printed much more quickly. In 1882 the *Graphic* had proudly announced that 'only ten years ago, if an event suitable for pictorial illustration occurred on the Saturday, it was considered sharp work to sketch, draw on the wood, engrave, electrotype, and print the subject to be illustrated on the following Saturday. By improved machinery it has become possible to illustrate an event happening on the Tuesday of the same week, and now we propose, by aid of the new electro-dynamo machines, to save many hours in electrotyping, and so be able to give our latest news pictures up to Wednesday evening.'

For a little while these improvements meant that for the first time the artist could communicate directly with the reader. Melton Prior's drawings were seldom tampered with, and were printed complete with their pencilled notes. The same was true for another talented artist of the later period, John Schönberg, an Austrian who worked chiefly for the *Illustrated London News* from 1866 until the Boxer Rebellion in 1900. Another artist with a distinctive style was Charlie Fripp who had a rather accident-prone career with the *Graphic* and *Daily Graphic* from 1879 until 1900. A new illustrated weekly, *Black and White*, commenced publication in Britain in 1890 and managed to maintain a high standard of reproduction in photographs and drawings. The paper's chief artists were René Bull and Charles Sheldon, whose adventurous life-styles were similar to those of the other great reporters of the golden period.

Unfortunately by the end of the century there was a distinct falling off in quality of illustrations in the pictorial press. Through no fault of the 'special artist', photography was becoming the dominant art, and it seemed the policy of many art editors to make an illustration look as much like a photograph as possible. There is a monotonous, grey look to the journals of the turn of the century. As action photography was not yet possible, for the sake of contrast a 'special's' sketches were redrawn in a more dramatic way by some distinguished artist at home. The *Sphere*, which was first published in 1900, had the majority of its sketches of the Boer War redrawn for publication. The profession of war illustrator was never quite the same after this, and before long photography took over almost completely.

The last decade of the nineteenth century was the high-noon in the life of the special war artist, before photography superseded illustration. In 1890 William Luson Thomas of the *Graphic* founded the first British daily picture paper, using photographic line blocks to reproduce the correspondent's sketches. In the *Daily Graphic*'s opening editorial he wrote: 'It has always been our intention to issue a daily paper illustrated, but it has only been by the gradual development of scientific processes, and improvement in the manufacture of paper and printing machinery that such an enterprise is rendered now possible.' Describing the Art Department of the new paper he said: 'Two or three rooms are occupied by the artists who are always in readiness to make sketches, at a moment's notice, in or out of the Studio. They have been trained here for months to draw for the quick processes, and were chosen out of a thousand applicants.' By 1890 newspapers could print an illustration within a few hours, although a 'special' at the Sudan took over three weeks to get his sketches back to England. The paper's two leading war artists were W. T. Maud and Charlie Fripp, whose sketches were used in their original form in the *Daily Graphic*, but were worked up by home-based artists for a more sumptuous presentation in the *Graphic*.

The *Daily Graphic* managed to keep up a very high standard of illustration considering the number of pictures that were needed daily. Many fine artists worked for the paper including R. Baden-Powell, who covered the Ashanti campaign, and on the home front, Paul Renouard, Reginald Cleaver, A. C. Corbould and Phil May. The paper carried an advertisement asking for amateurs to send in sketches of current events, in the same way as amateurs today send in photographs to newspapers, saying, 'The one all-important maxim is that of speedy despatch ... Indeed, nothing is more disappointing or irritating to the Artistic-Editor than to receive carefully worked-up Drawings or beautiful Photographs perhaps a day too late to prove of any use ... It must always be remembered that the Sketch should form the raw material which our artists at headquarters can understand and develop.' The paper continued in publication for nearly thirty years, when it was absorbed by the *Daily Sketch*. In 1904 the *Daily Mirror* was founded, and this was the first picture paper in the world to use only photographs. This was another nail in the coffin of the professional illustrator, although some papers, notably the *Illustrated London News*, continued to employ war artists up to the present day.

Apart from the Indian Wars, some of which were covered by Frederic Remington and Theodore R. Davis, America had little need of war artists after the Civil War until the Spanish–American War of 1898. Remington, best known for his pictures of the old West, was with Nelson A. Miles in his last campaign against the Navajo. His pictures were lively, told a story and were meticulously accurate. All his illustrations have the feeling of being drawn on the spot, coloured by a strong romantic feeling for the legend of the West. He said of his work, 'I paint for boys, boys from ten to seventy.' In 1898 he represented *Harper's* and the *New York Journal* at the Spanish–American War, seeing action at El Caney and San Juan Hill. At San Juan he reported an incident when the party came under Spanish fire. 'Prussian, English, and Japanese correspondents, artists, all the news, and much high-class art and literature, were flushed, and went straddling up the hill.' Remington became a close friend of Theodore Roosevelt and helped to create the legend of Roosevelt as a soldier by painting the Rough Riders going into action with Roosevelt at their head.

The Spanish–American War was short but a large number of foreign as well as American correspondents saw action there. William Dinwiddie of the *Washington Star* described the scene as they left Tampa for action in Cuba. 'It was a motley assembly which scurried through the hotel, in canvas hunting suits, in white ducks, in the brown fatigue clothes of the army, and even in immaculate white shirt fronts and patent leathers. Six-shooters, machetes and belts full of ammunition circulated through the halls, while broad shoulders were strung with shoulder straps from which dangled canteens, rolls of blankets, binoculars, kodaks and pouches filled with notebooks.' The American war artists included William Glackens, who was under contract to supply pictures for *McClure's Magazine* but became ill, and many of his pictures arrived too late for publication. *Leslie*'s 'specials' included Howard Chandler Christy, and Charles Sheldon, an American who had previously been working for *Black and White* in England.

Although heroes in their day, most nineteenth-century war illustrators have now been completely forgotten. When their active days in the field were over some became staff artists at home, a few became painters in their own right, while others took up book illustration, but for the most part they have been totally ignored in art histories. This may be because it was always difficult to judge how much of the finished reproduction in a journal was the artist's own work. Their case was somewhat similar to that of photographers: the technical processes came between the artist and the viewer, and the works of a war illustrator, like those of a photographer, did not seem to qualify for inclusion in the category of the fine arts. In fact the work of the best of the 'specials' was far superior to that of many Royal Academy war artists who painted from imagination. In the twentieth century, too, the nature of warfare changed. Writing after the First World War, Sir Philip Gibbs said, 'When Frederic Villiers began his career it was a different way of life. War was always terrible, but not so mechanical as this last War, and the correspondent was a more romantic figure, more dependent on his own resources, initiative, daring, imagination and audacity.' Photographers replaced illustrators almost completely, and the war artists sent by the Government to the front in the First World War fulfilled an entirely different function.

The American Civil War had produced some of the best drawings by artists in the front line but the apogee of war illustration as a profession was reached in the Sudan campaign. The 'specials' had become heroic figures and their work appealed to British sentiments of patriotism and imperialism. Victorian artistic conventions also favoured a picture that told a story and pointed a moral. Holman Hunt once said, 'Art should be a handmaid in the cause of Justice and Beauty.' Nothing very unpleasant was seen in the drawings, and everything was viewed through a romantic haze. In *The Light that Failed* Kipling outlined his belief that an illustrated journal's purpose was to supply the masses' demand for 'picturesqueness and abundance of detail; for there is more joy in England over a soldier who insubordinately steps out of square to rescue a comrade than over twenty generals slaving even to baldness at the gross details of transport and commissariat.' Popular literature followed the same pattern, dominated by the works of Kipling and G. A. Henty, both of whom had been war correspondents. The *Boy's Own Paper* and other comics carried drawings of heroic deeds in the cause of Empire very similar to those which appeared in the journals for adults. The romantic image of war held by those who did not fight was finally shattered in 1914, and the realistic art of photography took over so far as news was concerned. The appetite for a romantic story of warfare was catered for by the cinema, and the public enjoyed the epics of D. W. Griffiths and Cecil B. De Mille in the same way that their fathers and grandfathers had enjoyed following the adventures of Melton Prior and the other great war illustrators.

NOTES

[1] Joseph Hatton, *Journalistic London*.
[2] Frederic Villiers, *Pictures of Many Wars*.
[3] *Illustrated London News*, 10 May 1879.
[4] *Autobiography of William Simpson*.

Bibliography

Andrews, J. Cutler, *The North Reports the War*, 1954.

Bliss, Douglas Percy, *A History of Wood Engraving*, 1928.

Borcke, Johann von, *Memoirs of the Confederate War for Independence*, 1866.

Brown, Dee, *Bury My Heart at Wounded Knee*, 1970

Bullard, F. Lauriston, *Famous War Correspondents*, 1914.

Carter, A. C. R., *Work of War Artists in South Africa*, 1900.

Catton, Bruce, *The Coming Fury*, 1962. *Terrible Swift Sword*, 1963. *Never Call Retreat*, 1966.

Comaroft, John L., Ed., *Diary of Sol T. Plaatje*, 1973.

Crowe, Sir Joseph, *Reminiscences of Thirty-Five Years of My Life*, 1895.

Davis, Richard Harding, *Cuba in War Time*, 1897. *The Cuban and Porto Rican Campaign*, 1899.

Davis, Webster, *John Bull's Crime*, 1901.

Dawson, William Forrest, *A Civil War Artist at the Front*, 1957.

Donald, David, *Divided We Fought*, 1952.

Forbes, Archibald, *Memories and Studies of War and Peace*, 1895.

Freidel, Frank, *The Splendid Little War*, 1958.

Furniss, Harry, *My Bohemian Days*, 1919.

Gernsheim, Helmut and Alison, *Roger Fenton, Photographer of the Crimea*, 1954.

Griffith, Kenneth, *Thank God We Kept the Flag Flying*, 1974.

Hall, Sydney Prior, *Sketches from an Artist's Portfolio*, 1875. *Adventures in Many Lands*, 1879.

Hatton, Joseph, *Journalistic London*, 1882.

Hoole, William S., *Vizetelly Covers the Confederacy*, 1957.

Horgan, Paul, *Artists on Horseback*, 1972.

Jackson, Mason, *The Pictorial Press : Its Origin and Progress*, 1885.

Ketchum, Richard M., *American Heritage Picture History of the Civil War*, 1960.

Kipling, Rudyard, *The Light that Failed*, 1890.

Lynch, George, *Impressions of a War Correspondent*, 1902.

MacCracken, Harold, *Frederic Remington*, 1947.

Mathews, Joseph J., *Reporting the Wars*, 1957.

Miles, N. A., *Personal Recollections*, 1896.

Montagu, Irving, *Wanderings of a War Artist*, 1889. *Camp and Studio*, 1890.

Nevinson, Henry Wood, *Ladysmith : Diary of a Siege*, 1900.

Preston, Adrian, Ed., *In Relief of Gordon*, 1967.

Prior, Melton, *Campaigns of a War Correspondent*, 1912.

Reid, Forrest, *Illustrators of the Sixties*, 1928.

Reitz, Deneys, *Commando*, 1929.

Roosevelt, Theodore, *The Rough Riders*, 1899.

Rose, W. K., *With the Greeks in Thessaly*, 1897.

Russell, William Howard, *My Diary North and South*, 1863–5.

Sala, George Augustus, *My Diary in America in the Midst of War*, 1899.

Selby, John, *The Paper Dragon*, 1968.

Sheppard, Nathan, *Shut up in Paris*, 1871.

Simpson, William, *Seat of the War in the East*, 1856. *Autobiography of William Simpson*, 1903.

Stanley, Henry M., *Magdala*, 1896.

Steevens, George W., *With Kitchener to Khartoum*, 1898. *From Capetown to Ladysmith*, 1900.

Stern, Philip van Doren, *They were There*, 1959.

Stewart, Frank Algernon, *Cross Country with Hounds*, 1936.

Taft, Robert, *Artists and Illustrators of the Old West*, 1953.

Twyman, Michael, *Printing 1770–1970*, 1970.

Villiers, Frederic, *Pictures of Many Wars*, 1902. *Peaceful Personalities and Warriors Bold*, 1907. *Villiers : His Five Decades of Adventure*, 1920.

Wolseley, Garnet, *The Story of a Soldier's Life*, 1903.

Wright, H. C. Seppings, *The Soudan*, 1897. *Two Years Under the Crescent*, 1913.

The Illustrations

JOSEPH ARCHER CROWE (1825–96)
'Attack of the Russians on the heights of Balaclava', 25 and 26 October 1854
1853–6 CRIMEAN WAR
Original Watercolour
National Army Museum

'The special artist may be said to have commenced his career with the Crimean War' (*Illustrated London News*, 16 August 1879). One of the first of the 'specials', J. A. Crowe, had worked as a reporter on the *Daily News* between 1846 and 1852, and was also an accomplished artist and art historian. In 1854 he received a letter from Charles Mackay, then editor of the *Illustrated London News*: 'Can you start instantly for the seat of war for the *Illustrated London News*, and send us sketches and letters. I saw Thackeray just now, who says you sketch well. Let me know immediately. There will be no difficulty about liberal payment.' (Quoted in Sir Joseph Crowe's *Reminiscences of Thirty-five Years of My Life*.) The assignment interested him and he left immediately for the Crimea, reaching Balaclava in September 1854. On arrival he called on an old friend of his father's,

General Sir George De Lacy Evans who commanded the 2nd Division, and who gave him quarters in the lines of the 95th Regiment. De Lacy Evans also presented him with six bottles of port.

The Russians attacked Balaclava on the morning of 25 October in an attempt to relieve Sebastopol. An engraving of Crowe's watercolour appeared in the *Illustrated London News* of 11 November, with a note from the artist saying, 'I am sorry to be obliged to send you so little in the shape of sketches this week, but I have been in two actions, which are two days lost for writing or drawing; and today I have spent giving you an account of the battles. I shall endeavour to make up for this by next mail.' Crowe had a good view of the battle and saw the Light Brigade charge. At one stage, when with the Inniskilling Dragoons, he came under Russian fire. 'Now and then a shell from the Russian field-pieces came bowling along. One of them burst under my horse's belly, and took him off his legs. I manfully held on, with my sketch-book in one hand, my reins in the other, no harm done.'

JOSEPH ARCHER CROWE
'Our artist on the battlefield of Inkerman',
4–5 November 1854
1853–6 CRIMEAN WAR
Wood engraving
Illustrated London News, 3 February 1855, p. 116 top

Crowe accompanied the 95th Regiment at the Battle of Inkerman in November 1854. He wrote, 'There was quite a cannonade now going on without as yet much response on our side. It was dark, but I could see the fuses of the shells passing me; and one I observed, as I looked back, entering my tent.' On being ordered back to camp by Colonel Percy Herbert he had to thread an uneasy path through the Russian fire. 'I watched the shot as they came, and stopped or jumped to dodge them. . . . Lord Raglan, who did not know me, asked sternly what I was doing in that place. I said, "I am an artist", and showed him my sketch-book, in which were scraps of the battle.' On his return to camp Crowe requisitioned a new tent, and found that only one out of his six bottles of port was intact.

On 5 November, after the Russians had retreated, he crossed the battlefield, as shown in this engraving from one of his sketches. He wrote, 'I know nothing more fearful than a field of battle the day after the fight. . . . On horseback or on foot it was impossible to pass along without treading on the wounded or the dead, so thickly was the ground covered with them.' A sergeant said: 'The worst I felt was, when I came home and found all my comrades missing, and did not know whether they were dead or wounded; but had to go amongst the dead and wounded in the dark to see whom we could find.' After Crowe returned to camp he met *The Times* correspondent, William Russell, who had also been making notes on the battlefield, and gave him a glass of port from his remaining bottle. 'He found it delicious, and before I could partake of more than one glass for company's sake, he had drained the whole of it, without waiting.'

JOSEPH ARCHER CROWE
'Interior of the Malakoff, 9 September 1855'
1853–6 CRIMEAN WAR
Original watercolour
National Army Museum

Crowe got frostbite during one of the cold nights after the battle of Inkerman and had to return to England for surgery. He missed the severe winter of 1854–5 in the Crimea and instead lectured in London on the course of the war. Ingram of the *Illustrated London News* was anxious for him to return to the front and he got back to the Crimea in June 1855. The final bombardment of Sebastopol commenced on 5 September, the city and its forts falling three days later.

The fall of the Malakoff was not announced in the *Illustrated London News* until 15 September, and on 22 September a highly imaginative illustration of the event was provided by Gustav Doré. The first more realistic engraving, based on a sketch by Crowe, did not appear in the journal until 13 October. Crowe described how, after the battle was over, he 'entered the Redan almost over the corpses of the slain.' After making careful drawings, he moved on to the Malakoff. Here 'the place was occupied by Chasseurs-à-pièd. On a mound there waved the French and British standards. I sketched the remains of the tower, which had been for so many months the object of our wonder and admiration, and which we had seen, as it were, crumbling daily under the fire of the allied cannon. . . . The traverses were all ragged and torn, fascines and gabions thrown over or out of place, bags torn from position in which they had stood when shot. . . . It was late before I got back to my tent. I had many drawings and gathered information in quantities.' He sent off the material the next day and his report reached London on 22 September. 'No other correspondent had had similar good fortune.'

Crowe remained in the Crimea until peace was signed. As winter came he found his 'watercolour brushes stick to the paper as the tints turned to icicles.' After the war his life changed. He became superintendent of an art college in India, continued his work as an art historian, and acted as a correspondent in India and at the Austro-Italian War of 1859 for *The Times*. When he was thirty-four he entered the Foreign Office and pursued a distinguished career there.

JOSEPH ARCHER CROWE
'Interior of the Malakoff, 9 September 1855'
1853–6 CRIMEAN WAR
Wood engraving
Illustrated London News, 13 October 1855, p. 433

The engraver has added to Crowe's original
watercolour. More figures, possibly based on
other Crowe sketches, have been placed in the
right foreground and centre background, but
the general layout of the watercolour has been
followed.

EDWARD ANGELO GOODALL
(1819–1908)
'M. Soyer's camp and bivouac kitchen in the Crimea'
1853–6 CRIMEAN WAR

Wood engraving

Illustrated London News, 22 September 1855,
p. 348 top

E. A. Goodall was another artist engaged by the *Illustrated London News* to represent them at the Crimean War. He was a landscape artist who had exhibited at the Royal Academy and the Old Watercolour Society, and had been artist to the Guinea Boundary Commission in 1841. The photographer Roger Fenton, who was in the Crimea early in 1855, had critical words to say about Goodall's war drawings in a letter to William Agnew on 9 April 1855: 'His sketches which appear in the paper seem to astonish everyone from their total want of likeness to the reality' (Helmut and Alison Gernsheim, *Roger Fenton, Photographer of the Crimea*).

This picture is of interest as it shows the bivouac stoves brought to the front line by Alexis Soyer in an attempt to improve the food for fighting men. Soyer was chef to the Reform Club in London and had come to the Crimea at his own expense. On 27 August 1855 he demonstrated his new stove and kitchen to the army authorities. 'The scene was greatly enlivened by two military bands playing the whole of the time, amidst the roar of cannon and explosion of shells from Sebastopol and the trenches,' Soyer wrote. 'Seven of my camp stoves were placed in the open air on the esplanade in front of the Guards and Highlanders, containing the various specimens of food, recipes for which were distributed throughout the camp. The stoves are now in daily use by the Guards and Coldstream Company.' He hoped that when the rest of his equipment arrived 'the whole of the army will be able to cook under my new system, which is now recognized by all who witnessed it to be expeditious, clean and economical, especially in the consumption of fuel.'

Once the war was over Edward Goodall returned to a quiet life of painting and travelling abroad.

HON. AUGUSTUS MURRAY CATHCART

'My room at Erzurum'
1853–6 CRIMEAN WAR
Original watercolour
National Army Museum

There were a number of amateur artists among the soldiers at the Crimean War whose sketches were not meant for publication in the illustrated press. One of these painters was the Hon. Augustus Murray Cathcart, nephew of Sir George Cathcart, commander of the 4th Division. Augustus Cathcart had been commissioned in 1846 in the 93rd Sutherland Highlanders. At the start of the Crimean War he was made ADC to his uncle and served with him at the Alma, Balaclava and Inkerman. After Sir George was killed at Inkerman he became deputy assistant adjutant general attached to the Light Division. During this time he was sent to the Asia Minor front where the Turks defended the fortress of Kars against Russian attack. Erzurum

was the Turkish supply base for the area and Cathcart was probably stationed here from 1855 until the end of the war. Life was obviously more comfortable at Erzurum and his billet in a typical Turkish house looks pleasant. After the war the Turks awarded him the order of Medjidie 5th Class for his liaison work with them. Cathcart was made a lieutenant-colonel in 1856 and finally sold his commission in 1867.

WILLIAM SIMPSON (1823-99)

'Commissariat difficulties'

1853–6 CRIMEAN WAR

Original watercolour

Victoria and Albert Museum

Although William Simpson was a front-line
artist during the Crimean War, he was not there
as a journalist representing the illustrated press.
His job was to supply Colnaghi with paintings
for reproduction as a series of lithographs
entitled *The Seat of the War in the East*.

The painting shows the village of Kadikoi on
the road between Balaclava and the camp during
the storms in November 1854. William Russell
described the weather in *The Times*: 'Rain kept
pouring down – the skies were black as ink – the
wind howled over the staggering tents – the
trenches were turned into dikes – in the tents the
water was sometimes a foot deep – our men had
neither warm nor waterproof clothing – they
were plunged into the inevitable miseries of a
winter campaign – and not a soul seemed to care
for their comfort, or even for their lives.' It was
difficult to get food up from Balaclava as the
country roads had become impassable and no
road works had been done to improve them. The
food, marooned in the ships, was tossed about or
lost at sea. The Commissariat was completely
incapable of dealing with the magnitude of the
problem. It was not until the spring that things
began to get better, and the army's winter
clothing finally came through after the weather
got warmer. Some of the waggons in Simpson's
picture are taking the sick to Balaclava.

44

WILLIAM SIMPSON
'Huts and warm clothing for the Army'
1853-6 CRIMEAN WAR
Lithograph from The Seat of the War in the East (*Plate 16 1st Series*) *Paul and Dominic Colnaghi National Army Museum*

November storms had blown down the soldiers' tents and more suitable accommodation was needed for the winter months. After the torrential rain came the snow. Simpson wrote in his *Autobiography*, 'The sufferings of the troops during the winter roused the feelings of the people at home, and all sorts of things were sent out. But nothing could make men comfortable in the trenches, or even in the camp, while rain, snow, and frost continued.' The usual pattern was for rain to fall during the day. 'Before midnight the rain would change to snow; and before morning, it would be a hard frost. The men must have been first wet through and then frozen into icicles.' In January, William Russell reported that the valley and plateau of Balaclava 'were of a blanched white, seamed and marked by lines of men and horses carrying up provisions. . . . The trenches were two or three feet deep with mud, snow and half-frozen slush. . . . On the 16th the thermometer was at 14° in the morning and at 10° on the heights over Balaclava. The snow fell at night, and covered the ground to a depth of three feet.' Sometimes the drifts mounted up to five or six feet.

Simpson's picture shows the snow now covering the road from Balaclava to the front. The men wear a mixture of clothing acquired somehow or other to keep them warm until the arrival of army supplies. Simpson writes, 'This drawing is no caricature of life as it appeared during the winter season in the Crimea. The strange looking animal in the foreground is a mule laden with buffalo-hides; behind which is a soldier bearing sheepskin cloaks; the Hussar behind him is one of Lord Cardigan's regiment.' Further up the line going towards the front is a member of the Heavy Cavalry, pulling the starving mules into the camp, 'laden with wood for the huts'. The man carrying coats, shoes and flannel comforters is one of the Guards.

WILLIAM SIMPSON
'Embarkation of the sick at Balaclava'
1853–6 CRIMEAN WAR
Lithograph from The Seat of the War in the East (*Plate
23 1st Series*) *Paul and Dominic Colnaghi*
National Army Museum

The army sick and wounded were taken from the
front to Balaclava where there was a hospital,
and the most serious cases were sent on to
Scutari, Florence Nightingale's base. Simpson
mentions in his *Autobiography*, 'I was often
asked on my return about Miss Nightingale; but
she was always at Scutari.' The two never
met. Instead he mentions a Mrs Seacole, 'an
elderly mulatto woman from Jamaica', who was
one of the nurses at Balaclava when he was there.
'She had a taste for nursing and doctoring, but
she added to this a business as a sutler.'

The French helped to bring the sick down to
Balaclava, and mule trains could be seen during
the winter carrying the wounded to the harbour.
Mounted orderlies cleared the roads so that their
progress could be uninterrupted. 'So rapidly and
well was the whole duty performed, that the
writer has seen more than one hundred sick men
brought down to the wharf, removed from the
litters, and all of them embarked, in less than
half an hour,' wrote William Simpson.

The scene in the picture is 'Sick Wharf',
Balaclava, at the head of the harbour. Kadikoi is
in the background, with the General Hospital on
the right. Lieutenant Goss, the naval officer in
charge, is helping a sick soldier into the boat.
On the right is Dr Cortello and behind him Dr
Anderson. William Russell, who watched the
long processions of wounded going down to
Balaclava, wrote, 'They formed one of the most
ghastly processions that ever poet imagined.
Many of these men were all but dead. With
closed eyes, open mouths, and ghastly attenuated
faces, they were borne along two and two, the
thin stream of breath visible in the frosty air
alone showing that they were still alive.'

When Simpson returned to Britain, Colnaghi
held an exhibition of his paintings, which was
very popular as it was at this time 'quite a new
thing to have an artist at the seat of war depicting
events as they took place.'

WILLIAM SIMPSON
*'Return of the army from Magdala –
the mountain train'*
1867-8 ABYSSINIAN WAR
Wood engraving
Illustrated London News, 4 July 1868, p. 5

After the Crimean War, Simpson's next
expedition for Colnaghi's was to India in 1859 to
record the effects of the Mutiny. He travelled in
the country for some years but most of the
lithographic work for which he had been
commissioned was never printed because of the
collapse of the publishers.

He joined the *Illustrated London News* in 1866
as now 'the illustrated newspaper was taking the
place of the lithograph, and the wood-engraver
was supplanting the artist who drew on stone.'
At the outset of the British punitive expedition
to Abyssinia a serving officer, Colonel Baigre,
was used by the *Illustrated London News* as their
artist. 'But as the war went on the interest in it
increased, and as Baigre's sketches were only
landscapes, it was felt that someone who could
do figures should be sent out' (*Autobiography of
William Simpson*).

Simpson reached Annesley Bay on 25 March
1868, and there were 250 miles of extremely
rough country between him and Magdala. He set
out with 'horse, donkey, and two villainous-
looking servants' but did not reach Napier's
force until after Magdala was taken, King
Theodore dead and the expedition ready for the
return march. The engraving from his sketch
shows two batteries of small artillery on the
return journey. Each battery consisted of six
guns and every gun could be taken to pieces and
carried on the backs of mules. The journey was
difficult and 'no army has ever had such
obstacles to go over.' The line of troops in the
picture extended for seven or eight miles but the
artist was only able to show 'a bit of this length
of road covered with troops and baggage,' as he
told readers of the *Illustrated London News*. It
was a pity that Simpson had missed all the action
but he was able to give the general public some
idea of conditions in Abyssinia, and at the same
time to make many sketches of the people and
customs which could later be sold separately.

WILLIAM SIMPSON
'Arrest of English correspondents at Metz'
1870-1 FRANCO-PRUSSIAN WAR
Wood engraving
Illustrated London News, 20 August 1870, p. 192 top

After returning from Abyssinia, Simpson spent the next two years travelling abroad for the *Illustrated London News*. He was present at the opening of the Suez Canal, visited Jerusalem and made a return trip to the Crimea.

The journal next sent him to Paris when trouble between France and Germany appeared imminent and he arrived five days after war was declared. He travelled to Metz where many of the correspondents had assembled and here met Sydney Hall, who was representing the new British illustrated paper, the *Graphic*. Spy mania was at its height in Metz. Simpson and a colleague were mobbed by an angry crowd who saw him innocently sketching the Emperor's carriage. The French had just had two severe defeats at Wörth and Forbach and were looking for scapegoats. They suspected his sketchbook

'with its scraps of notes and bits of outline' and marched the two men through the town.

In wartime Simpson usually went to extreme cloak-and-dagger lengths to disguise the fact that he was an artist. 'A sketch-book was a most dangerous article to be found in your possession. . . . At Forbach the idea occurred to me of sketching on a book of cigarette papers. One could do a great deal on a book of that kind, and in the event of being apprehended, could make a cigarette of the sketch and smoke it before the eyes of one's accusers.' He sketched the Battle of Sedan on the back of a piece of wallpaper, the design of which could be seen through his finished sketch. He was at the siege of Strasbourg and later returned to Paris with the defeated French army. In Paris he was cautious when walking along the boulevards. 'If one did so, and opened his mouth, his words at once told he was a foreigner, and suspicious looks were the least result to be looked for.'

Defence of Paris, Cattle + Sheep in the Bois de Boulogne. Augt 1870. Wm Simpson.

WILLIAM SIMPSON
'The defence of Paris: cattle and sheep in the Bois de Boulogne'
1870–1 FRANCO-PRUSSIAN WAR
Original drawing
Pencil and wash
Victoria and Albert Museum

After the surrender of the French Emperor at Sedan, Simpson made his way back to Paris where the Parisians were preparing for the defence of the city. The *Illustrated London News* reported: 'At the present moment . . . the destruction of that beautiful resort of elegance and fashion, the Parc de Boulogne, is contemplated.' All public gardens were to be adapted for agriculture to provide food in case of a siege. 'There are prodigious herds of cattle and flocks of sheep in the Bois de Boulogne. These animals are allowed not only to graze, but to eat the leaves of the trees doomed to destruction.' Other city parks were scheduled for use in the same way, and 'twenty thousand sheep are to be penned in the Avenue de l'Imperatrice.' Defence works were also improvized.

Simpson's deceptively peaceful-looking sketch was reproduced as a wood engraving in the *Illustrated London News* on 10 September 1870. The description of it in the journal reads: 'As military necessity demands that the space commanded by the guns of a fortification should be clear, the trees on the glacis are ruthlessly sacrificed, to prevent their affording cover for the approach of an enemy; but the stumps are purposely left standing, with a few branches twined between them here and there, to form an abbattis. This is not high enough to give any cover, but a sufficient obstacle to the regular formation of the advancing troops.'

THE ILLUSTRATED LONDON NEWS.

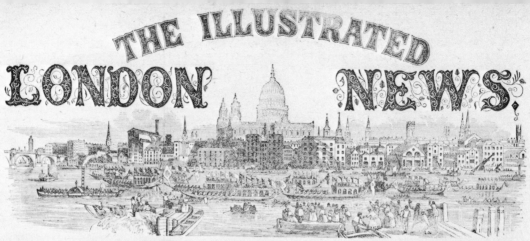

REGISTERED AT THE GENERAL POST-OFFICE FOR TRANSMISSION ABROAD.

No. 1648.—VOL. LVIII.   SATURDAY, APRIL 29, 1871.   PRICE FIVEPENCE
BY POST, 5½D.

WILLIAM SIMPSON
'A shell at Suresnes'
1871 PARIS COMMUNE
Wood engraving, redrawn by M. W. Ridley
Illustrated London News, 29 April 1871, p. 413

Simpson returned to France in April 1871 to record the struggles of the Commune accompanied by William Ingram, editor of the *Illustrated London News*. At Versailles while he was sketching, some shells from the Communards' guns 'came pretty near us' and some of the shells dropped short at Suresnes. After the bombardment Simpson went into the village to inspect the damage. While he was talking to some of the inhabitants a shell 'with a crash, went through a garret window, sending the fragments of glass about and blowing out the clean white window-blind, which fell fluttering to the ground. There was a rush of everyone to the house.' When the smoke and smell of 'villainous saltpetre' had subsided he managed to force his way upstairs. Here a man was standing in a dazed condition. The shell had come through the roof and straight through the floor to the room below without injuring anyone.

A few days after this incident Simpson obtained permission to enter Paris where he 'walked about during the day, going often to the outposts, where I seldom failed to find "incidents"'. During the 'Bloody Week' of 21–28 May he had several narrow escapes. Once he was standing with Dr Austin of *The Times* when a rifle bullet passed between them. Austin paid tribute to Simpson as being 'an old campaigner, who sketches as coolly under fire as in his own room'.

Simpson returned to London on 11 June. For the next few years he travelled abroad for the *Illustrated London News*, going with the Prince of Wales on his Indian tour and reporting on Schliemann's discoveries at Mycenae and Troy. His last campaign as a war artist was the 2nd Afghan War, 1878–80, where Archibald Forbes recalled seeing him 'on the day of Ali Musjid, as he stood sketching Sir Sam Browne's advancing brigade, with his back regardlessly to the Afghan fortress and the round shot and shell it was pouring forth' (*Graphic*, 6 December 1890). After this Simpson continued as an artist covering foreign stories for the *Illustrated London News*, and in 1892 was an honoured guest at the journal's Jubilee year celebration.

(Overleaf)
GEORGE ATKINSON (1822–59)
'Mutineers surprised by Her Majesty's 9th Lancers'
1857–9 INDIAN MUTINY
Lithograph from *The Campaign in India* published by Day & Co. (Plate 6)
National Army Museum

George Atkinson served with the Bengal Engineers from 1840 to 1859, and published a number of collections of lithographs on India: *Pictures from the North, in Pen and Pencil* (1848), *The Campaign in India* (1859) and *Curry and Rice* (1860). He was also the architect of the old Bengal Artillery Mess at Meirut.

This incident occurred in May 1857 in the early stages of the Indian Mutiny. General Anson at Ambala received orders to retake Delhi which had been captured by the mutineers, and

his troops moved off in the middle of May. Atkinson has shown an incident during the march when the force met a party of rebel sepoys making off with loot from Delhi and the adjoining stations. 'Mess plate, crockery, ladies' dresses etc etc were heaped rudely together, to be sorted and divided at some more fitting opportunity.' The Lancers surprised them before they had time to yoke their bullocks. 'That evening's sun sees that belt of trees with a rebel swinging from every bough. A drum-head court martial has convicted them one and all. A small native cart is brought under a tree – the rope is fastened to the rebel's neck and the overhanging branch – the cart is suddenly driven on, and the miscreant left to swing.' Atkinson's description accompanies the lithograph. His dramatic picture cannot have borne much relation to reality, although the uniforms and background were probably accurate.

GEORGE ATKINSON
'Wounded men at Dugshai'
1857–9 INDIAN MUTINY
Lithograph from *The Campaign in India* published by
Day & Co. (Plate 26)
National Army Museum

This Atkinson lithograph shows more signs of
being painted on the spot than the previous
illustration. It is typical of his distinctive style,
which even the wood engraver of the *Illustrated
London News* could not quite eliminate from the
sketches which he occasionally sent for
publication in the journal. Dugshai was in the
hills near Simla and a suitable place for a
hospital. An empty barracks, seen at the top
right of the picture, was adapted for the
reception of sick and wounded. 'Here men of the
Fusiliers, Artillery, Lancers, and other
regiments, were to be seen enjoying the truly

exhilarating air, after the terrific heat and
exposure to which they had been subjected.' The
barrack roof was covered in 'shingle', 'that is,
with strips of wood, laid on slate fashion, which
according to the back-wood American system, is
the prevailing kind of roofing in the Hills, where
timber is plentiful; the walls are of rubble
masonry.'

HENRY HOPE CREALOCK (1831–91)

'A skirmish with Tartar cavalry in the campaign of 1860'

1860 3RD CHINA WAR
Original drawing
Pencil
National Army Museum

Henry Hope Crealock was a soldier and also a talented artist who sent some of his sketches to the *Illustrated London News*, where they were published as wood engravings. Crealock was commissioned in the 90th Foot in 1848 and served with his regiment and on the staff during the Crimean War. He was sent to China in 1857 and again in 1860. A British and French expeditionary force set off in May 1860 with the intention of taking the Taku forts at the mouth of the River Peiho, and advancing on Peking. After landing at Peh-tang the army marched towards Sinho, and were harassed on the road by Tartar cavalry. The Tartars were skilled shots and rode on swift ponies. They captured some of the British soldiers, including the 'Private of the Buffs' celebrated in Sir Francis Hastings Doyle's poem, who was killed when he refused to bow to the Tartar Mandarin Sankolinsin. The expedition was successful, Peking occupied, and the Imperial Summer Palace destroyed.

HENRY HOPE CREALOCK
'Assault on Canton, 29 December 1857'
1856–9 2ND CHINA WAR
Original drawing
Pen and ink
National Army Museum

The Chinese Opium Wars between 1839 and 1860 arose out of a conflict of trade interests and resulted in the French and British attacking Canton in December 1857. After a preliminary bombardment, the troops landed and made for the wall of Canton, as shown in Crealock's sketch. The Chinese offered little resistance. *The*

Times reported, 'They seemed determined simply to ignore our presence here.' A few days later the British entered the city and captured the Imperial Commissioner, Yeh Ming-Ch'en. The Treaty of Tientsin, signed on 26 June 1858, brought this stage of the war to a close.

Crealock later served in India and fought at the Zulu War of 1879, where he completed a number of sketches. When stationed at home he specialized in sporting pictures.

FRANK VIZETELLY (d.1883)

'The revolution in Sicily: defence of the barricade at the Porta Felice: one of Garibaldi's officers planting the Italian flag'
1860–1 ITALIAN WARS OF UNIFICATION
Wood engraving
Illustrated London News, 16 June 1860, pp. 576–7

Frank Vizetelly's elder brothers Henry and James were both pioneers of the illustrated press in Britain. In his twenties Frank Vizetelly had worked for the *Pictorial Times*, an early competitor of the *Illustrated London News* which had been edited by his brother Henry, and in 1857 he helped his brother James found the French picture paper *Le Monde Illustré*. His first assignment as a 'special' for the *Illustrated London News* was to cover the war between Austria and Sardinia-Piedmont in 1857–8. In 1860 he joined Garibaldi and his red-shirts during the invasion of Sicily, arriving at Palermo on 22 May. Garibaldi reached the eastern gates on 27 May at dawn and by 10.00 a.m. the greater part of the town was in his hands. *The Times* correspondent wrote, 'One must know these Sicilians to have an idea of the frenzy, screaming, shouting, crying, and hugging; all would kiss his hands and embrace his knees' (8 June 1860).

Vizetelly's account of the action did not reach London for nearly three weeks as all post was stopped from Sicily and correspondence had to be got somehow to Malta or Naples for despatch. He was able to watch fierce street fighting on the morning of 27 May and described how 'the sure aim of Garibaldi's chasseurs tells fearfully on the dense masses of soldiery blocked in the narrow streets.' Barricades were thrown up by both sides and at the Porta Felice 'a barricade has been raised, and on it one of Garibaldi's officers plants the Italian flag amidst a storm of grapeshot.' Fighting continued throughout the night. 'There is little or no sleep to be obtained by even a non-combatant, who at any moment may be awakened by a live shell in his bed.' Vizetelly was able to meet Garibaldi before coming down with a fever on 7 June. 'I was so much about in the sun, and this, combined with the stench of the dead blocking the narrow streets in all directions, brought on an attack of fever that completely knocked me up for three days. I sat amongst a pile of dead for two hours or more at the White Benedictine Convent sketching the horrors there, and this, I believe, brought on the attack.'

FRANK VIZETELLY
'Stampede from Bull Run, 21 July 1861'
1861–5 AMERICAN CIVIL WAR
Wood engraving
Illustrated London News, 17 August 1861,
p. 167 bottom

Vizetelly did not return from Italy until the end of 1860. In May 1861 he arrived in America to represent the *Illustrated London News* at the Civil War. He resolved to 'enter into the merits of the quarrel' and find out why 'two branches of the same family' were fighting (15 June 1861). He joined the Federal side and witnessed their defeat at Bull Run in July, the first significant battle of the war. His illustration shows the Federal troops in full flight, pursued by the Virginian cavalry. 'Retreat is a weak term to use when speaking of this disgraceful rout, for which there was no excuse. The terror-stricken soldiers threw away their arms and accoutrements, herding along like a panic-stricken flock of sheep, with no order whatever in their flight. Those who had been fortunate enough to get placed in the baggage-wagons thrust back others with their bayonets and musket stocks. Wounded men were crushed under the wheels of the heavy, lumbering chariots that dashed down the road at full speed. Light buggies, containing members of Congress, were overturned or dashed to pieces in the horrible confusion of the panic.' William Russell of *The Times* was horrified as he watched McDowell's army in ignominious retreat. 'What is all this about?' he asked a Federal officer. 'Why, it means we are pretty badly whipped, that's the truth,' the officer replied.

In August 1861 Vizetelly tried to give his readers at home some idea of the hardships of a 'special's' life when not in the firing line. 'There are many, no doubt, who on reading a correspondent's letter envy him the life of excitement he is supposed to lead with an army in the field. . . . They picture to themselves the air filled with martial music, the march through shady forests in the 'old dominion' of Virginia, the occasional halts amidst romantic scenery, the bath at some crystal spring. . . . Such, my friends, is the romance of campaigning; read on, and you will see reality.' The true state of affairs was that he was plagued by mosquitoes, had rattlesnakes in his boots and the only washing facilities were in 'this main sewer of a clayey range of hills' (3 August 1861).

FRANK VIZETELLY

'My reconnaissance with General Sickles in the Potomac'

1861–5 AMERICAN CIVIL WAR
Wood engraving
Illustrated London News, 7 December 1861,
p. 570 bottom

In August 1861 Vizetelly was with the Federal camp on the Potomac, fifty miles below Washington. The Confederates had batteries on the lower river which stopped merchant ships getting through, partially blockading the capital. The Federal intention was to bombard the Confederate batteries from their own position at Budds' Ferry.

Vizetelly went with the General's reconnaissance party and they observed several small Confederate ships attempting to run the blockade. 'During my visit a dozen or so of small schooners of light draught successfully ran the blockade by hugging the Maryland shore closely, where the water shoals considerably. . . . We on our side watched the little ships anxiously as they came within range of the enemy's gun, which they no sooner did than a terrible fire of shot and shell opened upon them, not one, however, being struck seriously, and all enabled to keep their course down the river. We, the spectators, ran probably more risk than the vessels, for many of the shells came over to our neighbourhood, bursting in close proximity to where we stood. Our turn then came and we gave them a few rounds from the tiny Parrotts, pitching the 10-pound shells right into their works, and peppering a steamer.'

Vizetelly found the reconnaissance trip an exciting experience. The party waded along the bed of the Potomac for much of the way, and were forced to swim their horses in the water as the river bank was impassable in many places. In the sketch the party has reached Indian Head, close to the batteries, and the artist is second from the left.

FRANK VIZETELLY
'Jefferson Thompson's guerillas shooting at Federal boats on the Mississippi'
1861–5 AMERICAN CIVIL WAR
Wood engraving
Illustrated London News, 14 June 1862, p. 599

In January 1862 Vizetelly obtained permission to accompany General Burnside's Roanoke Island expedition and on 28 February he described the Federal victory there. Next he had a short spell with General McClellan's army in Virginia. William Russell of *The Times* was also present, and when the Secretary of War, Edwin M. Stanton, revoked the correspondents' permits, Russell left for London in a huff and Vizetelly transferred to the western campaign, joining General Halleck's advance on Corinth. Halleck was also hostile to correspondents and wanted all civilians excluded from the army lines. Vizetelly had now to provide his own transport and was very indignant.

Jefferson Thompson was an active guerilla commander who caused trouble for the Federal army in Missouri and on the Mississippi. This area was the economic centre of the Confederacy, containing the cotton states and the great ports and cities. The Federals found it easier to advance by river as they were less vulnerable to surprise attack.

Vizetelly writes: 'This incident happened to the boat on which I have established my headquarters, and the attempt was made on her from the Arkansas shore just above the first Chickasaw Bluff. We distinctly saw the rascals, and a strong party was put on shore to capture them, if possible, but they were too well acquainted with the woods, and escaped. We risk at any moment being fired into from the bank; and the unfortunate individual who would attempt to land alone and unarmed on a foraging expedition is almost certain to fall into the hands of these ruffians, for such they should be called from their acts. The chivalrous Southern Confederacy does not appear particular as to the means it employs to attain its ends.'

FRANK VIZETELLY
'Cotton burners in the neighbourhood of
Memphis surprised by Federal scouts'
1861–5 AMERICAN CIVIL WAR
Wood engraving
Illustrated London News, 9 August 1862, p. 149

Vizetelly returned to Washington in June 1862 as
he had heard that he might obtain a pass to join
the Army of the Potomac on the James River.
Meanwhile his admiration had been growing for
the South. On 4 July he wrote: 'I never saw
anything of Southern people until I landed at
Memphis. . . . If the entire South is actuated by
the same sentiments breathed by the people of
south-western Tennessee and Mississippi, why,
then I declare the reconstruction of the Union
impossible.'

This is one of his last sketches from the
Federal side and based on his experiences with
Halleck's army at Memphis. The only
excitement at this time had been the 'occasional
collision between scouting parties of Indiana
cavalry and the guerilla bands of cotton burners'
who were anxious that their supplies should not
get into enemy hands when the city fell. 'We
came across a party of Southerners on a
plantation destroying every bale they could lay
their hands on. In the foreground an officer is
"hurrying up" the business; one man applies the
torch to a pile of loose cotton; others are ripping
open and rolling up the bales; while a group of
frightened whites and negroes are assembled
under the porch of the house. We took two or
three of the guerilla band; the rest scattered and
made for the surrounding timber.'

At last, tired of waiting for his correspondent's
pass from the Federal authorities, Vizetelly
decided to join the Confederacy. He crossed the
Potomac in company with a negro called Job,
having a hazardous time avoiding Federal patrol
boats, and made his way to Richmond. Here he
joined Robert E. Lee's march along the Rapidan.

FRANK VIZETELLY
'Night amusements in the Confederate camp'
1861–5 AMERICAN CIVIL WAR
Wood engraving
Illustrated London News, 10 January 1863,
p. 40 bottom

Vizetelly's first drawing from the Confederate side was 'General Stuart with his cavalry in the neighbourhood of Culpeper Courthouse' which appeared in the *Illustrated London News* on 4 October 1862. He commented on the rough, worn appearance of the men and their equipment, 'consisting mainly of old rusty sabres and shot-guns', caused by the Federal blockade. 'As it is, they are the finest irregular body of horse in the world.' He described how 'every evening, when we cluster around our pine-log fire, the darkies press in amongst us and listen to the yarns their masters spin. In our camp we are fortunate enough to possess the most famous banjo-player in the Southern States,' and when he strikes up he will 'put his legs through a series of marvellous gyrations, to the delight of the

sympathetic lookers-on, who beat time for him. Although the enemy is within cannon-shot, no one experiences the least uneasiness, and the universal refrain is, "We'll sing tonight and fight tomorrow – bullyboys Oh!"'

Major Heros von Borcke was with Vizetelly at this time and also mentions the scenes of camp life which 'Vizetelly's clever pencil has placed before the European public in the pages of the *Illustrated London News*. Less successful was our friend in his efforts to improve the cuisine of our negro camp cook, and we often had the laugh on him – especially when one day he produced in triumph a roast pig, with the conventional apple in his mouth, which we found to be raw on one side and burnt to a cinder on the other' (*Memoirs of the Confederate War for Independence*).

Little of Vizetelly's material got through to the *Illustrated London News* during the summer of 1862, and he rightly suspected the Federal picture papers of using his sketches for their own pages.

FRANK VIZETELLY

*'Southern refugees in the woods near
Vicksburg'*

1861–5 AMERICAN CIVIL WAR

Wood engraving

Illustrated London News, 29 August 1863, p. 216 top

Vicksburg held out against the Federals until 4
July 1863 when Grant entered the city, giving
the Union control of the entire Mississippi valley
and cutting the Confederacy in two. During the
siege the inhabitants had suffered constant
shelling and lack of food. A Vicksburg woman
wrote, 'I have never understood before the full
force of these questions – what shall we eat?
what shall we drink? and wherewithal shall we
be clothed?' A Missouri soldier believed that you
could hardly tell the difference between mule
meat and beef when it was cooked correctly.

Vizetelly was outside Vicksburg during the
siege but volunteered to go some of the way with
a party trying to get ammunition supplies into
the city. One of his sketches shows the party who
had braved the Federal pickets. This picture
shows what happened to some of the inhabitants
of the town after it was taken by the Federals.

'The country for forty miles round Vicksburg is
covered with small encampments of women and
children who have been driven from their homes
by predatory bands of Northern soldiers. . . .
With nothing but a few yards of canvas to
protect them from the frequent thunderstorms
which burst in terrific magnificence at this season
of the year over Mississippi, they support with
dignity their heavy trial. A cavalry soldier has
just come into the camp with letters, and has
given animation to the illustration.'

After the fall of Vicksburg Vizetelly returned
to Charleston. At this period he was experiencing
difficulty in obtaining the sketching materials he
needed, because of the Federal blockade.

FRANK VIZETELLY
'The Federals shelling the city of Charleston'
1861–5 AMERICAN CIVIL WAR
Wood engraving
Illustrated London News, 5 December 1863,
p. 561 bottom

From September to November 1863 communication between Vizetelly and the offices of the *Illustrated London News* in London ceased. This was not the fault of the artist who was regularly sending sketches off. The *Illustrated London News* thought that some of his 'packages were doomed to the Gulf Stream, whilst others fall into the hands of Federal cruisers, whence his sketches find their way occasionally into the pages of the illustrated journals of New York.' This picture did in fact appear in *Harper's Weekly*, and was published in the *Illustrated London News* nearly five months after the event.

Vizetelly was inside Charleston when the Federals started a new bombardment in July 1863. General Gillmore had a gun known as 'Swamp Angel' trained on the city firing 200 pound shells. A new type of incendiary shell was also used with the hope of starting fires. Vizetelly later wrote that 'sick and bedridden people' were carried from their homes 'on mattresses, and mothers with infants in their arms running they knew not whither' when the guns started up (*Cornhill Magazine*, July 1864). 'All through the night we could hear the screams and groans of the wounded lying within a few yards of us; but as a continual fire was kept up by the advanced pickets it was impossible to do anything for them without running great risk of being shot.' The Confederate General Beauregard protested to the Federal commander at the number of non-combatants who were being killed, and there was a twenty-four hour truce during which some of them were evacuated. Mercifully 'Swamp Angel' exploded after firing thirty-six shots, and Charleston stood firm until February 1864.

In January Vizetelly returned to England, but was back in September in the Shenandoah area. After the war he continued as a 'special' for the *Illustrated London News*, covering the Prussian–Austrian War of 1866 and the Carlist Rising of 1868. He went to Egypt on behalf of the *Graphic* in 1882 and was presumed killed after the Mahdists captured El Obeid on 17 January 1883, massacring a British force under Colonel William Hicks.

ALFRED R. WAUD (1828–91)

'The Army of the Potomac: burying the dead and burning dead horses at Fair Oaks Station, Virginia, 31 May 1862'

1861–5 AMERICAN CIVIL WAR
Original drawing
Pencil and chinese white
Library of Congress

Al Waud was leading special artist for *Harper's Weekly* during the American Civil War. Waud was born in London where he studied art, and later spent some time as a scene-painter. He came to America in 1850 with his brother William, who also became an illustrator. An album of Al Waud's work is at the Library of Congress, and the sketches have a freshness and ferocity which the engravers never caught.

During the first year of the war Waud worked for Barnum and Beach's *Illustrated News*, seeing action at Bull Run where he got a lift in Matthew Brady's photographic wagon, having to contend with breaking photographic plates and bottles of chemicals when the horses bolted under bombardment on the battlefield.

Accredited to *Harper's* in 1862, Waud joined General McClellan's Peninsular Campaign in May. The same month the Chickahominy River flooded after violent storms, and McClellan was caught with part of his army on the north side, while General Erasmus Keyes and the IV Corps had crossed and were isolated on the far side at Fair Oaks, a railway depot, the name of which came from the oak plantations surrounding the two houses in the sketch. Seizing his chance, the Confederate General Johnston attacked Fair Oaks on 31 May, but after two days' fighting and heavy casualties the result was indecisive. According to one Massachusetts soldier, after Fair Oaks the soil seemed to have 'the damp, mouldy odor' of blood. 'The surgeons were at work cutting off legs and arms with the most businesslike air, and near by the rebel dead, to the number of hundreds, perhaps, were being buried in a long trench, where they were laid without mark or distinction, side by side, and covered with four or five feet of earth decently and without injury' (T. L. Livermore, *Days and Events*). General Johnston was wounded in the battle and replaced by Robert E. Lee.

A advancing to the capture of disabled guns Gaines Mills

ALFRED R. WAUD
'Confederates overrun a disabled Federal battery at Gaines' Mill'
1861–5 AMERICAN CIVIL WAR
Original drawing
Pencil and chinese white
Library of Congress

Robert E. Lee was determined to turn the Confederate army inherited from Johnston into an efficient fighting force. He improved the defences of Richmond and sent out General 'Jeb' Stuart on a reconnaissance mission to report on the weak points of McClellan's position, between White Oak swamps and Mechanicsville. Stuart reported that the Federal right flank was unprotected as was the depot at the White House. Lee recalled Stonewall Jackson from the Shenandoah Valley and made plans for an attack which commenced on 26 June 1862 and went on until 1 July, later to be known as the Seven Days Battle. One of the actions was at Gaines' Mill where A. P. Hill led the Confederate advance at noon on 27 June. Reinforcements arrived with Stonewall Jackson and Harvey Hill late in the evening and the Confederates were at last able to gain ground.

Reporting the battle, the *Harper's* correspondent wrote, 'By two o'clock the woods covering the hill were thronged by the two contending armies. The enemy generally advanced in three lines, the first firing and falling down while that behind repeated the same movement. . . . The fiercest portion of the fight was near the brow of the hill. Batteries thundered, musketry roared, and the din and noise of the contending forces were terrific.'

McClellan reported, 'Another day of desperate fighting. We are hard pressed by superior numbers. I fear that I shall be forced to abandon my material to save my men under cover of the gunboats. . . . My army has behaved superbly, and have done all that men can do. If none of us escape, we shall at least have done honor to the country' (Official Records of the War of the Rebellion, Vol. XI). McClellan withdrew, leaving the wounded behind at Savage's Station. Lee informed the Confederate President Jefferson Davis that 'after a severe contest of five hours' the enemy had been put to flight.

Waud's drawing shows the battlefield in the evening after the Confederate advance.

Saturday, August 30th 1862   Defeat of the Army   of Genl

ALFRED R. WAUD
'2nd Bull Run, 30 August 1862: a Union battery firing canister at point-blank range, tries to check the charge against the Union left wing, while a mounted officer attempts to rally his fleeing men'
1861–5 AMERICAN CIVIL WAR
Original drawing
Pencil, wash and chinese white
Library of Congress

The Federal army under General Pope attacked Stonewall Jackson's line, which was drawn up beside the stream of Bull Run, on 28 August 1862. Jackson, supported by A. P. Hill, held out and by the evening of the second day Longstreet's men had come up to support him on the right flank. Pope's despatch written on 30 August said: 'We fought a terrific battle here yesterday with the combined forces of the enemy, which lasted with continuous fury from daylight until after dark, by which time the enemy was driven from the field, which we now occupy' (*Harper's Weekly*, 13 September 1862). On the third day the Confederate artillery bombarded the advancing Union troops and a counter-attack was launched under Longstreet's command. Pope retreated into Centreville, but exhaustion and rain prevented the Confederates pressing home their advantage. Waud's drawing shows the retreat.

A Confederate soldier who survived the battle wrote: 'Oh, the horrid scenes around us! Brains, fractured skulls, broken arms and legs, and the human form mangled in every conceivable and inconceivable manner' (J. T. Durkin, *John Dooley, Confederate Soldier*). The *Tribune* correspondent said, 'I believe there cannot be a man who heard or participated in that awful tragedy but counts the hour between $4\frac{1}{2}$ and $5\frac{1}{2}$ o'clock the severest fighting he ever knew.... By half after five it was apparent that we were beaten – outflanked by a concentration upon the left.'

Waud was taken prisoner by the rebels during or soon after the fighting.

Previous to Antietam

74

ALFRED R. WAUD

'Federal pickets observe Lee crossing the Potomac river on a moonlit night early in September 1862'
1861–5 AMERICAN CIVIL WAR
Original drawing
Wash and chinese white
Library of Congress

The Confederates were near to victory in September 1862. Now Lee invaded the North. He was convinced that the Marylanders would rise in his support, and the army crossed the Potomac thirty miles upstream from Washington and entered Northern territory.

Waud was still a prisoner of the Confederates and *Harper's Weekly* published a drawing of his of the 1st Virginia Cavalry on 27 September. Waud said, 'Being detained within the enemy's lines, an opportunity occurred to make a sketch of one of the two crack regiments of the Confederate service.'

The same issue of *Harper's* reports the rebel invasion. 'The rebels appear to have begun their crossing on the 4th, and to have thrown bodies of men steadily forward ever since. The artillery crossed on a pontoon bridge, the cavalry and infantry forded the stream, the water being knee and thigh deep. . . . The rebels are wretchedly clad, and generally destitute of shoes. The cavalry men are mostly barefooted, and the feet of the infantry are bound up in rags and pieces of rawhide. Their uniforms are in tatters, and many are without hats or caps. They are very sanguine of success, and say that when they get to Baltimore they will get everything they need.'

Heros von Borcke, who crossed with Lee, later described the scene in his memoirs. 'It was, indeed, a magnificent sight as the long column of many thousand horsemen stretched across this beautiful Potomac. The evening sun slanted upon its clear placid waters, and burnished them with gold, while the arms of the soldiers glittered and blazed in its radiance. There were few moments, perhaps, from the beginning, to the close of the war, of excitement more intense, of exhilaration more delightful, than when we ascended the opposite bank to the familiar but now strangely thrilling music of "Maryland my Maryland".'

Waud's beautiful drawing does not appear to have been published in *Harper's*.

ALFRED R. WAUD

'Carrying off the wounded after the battle of Antietam'

1861–5 AMERICAN CIVIL WAR
Wood engraving
Harper's Weekly, 11 October 1862, p. 649

One of the more successful wood engravings from a Waud sketch, this picture was accompanied by a written report from the correspondent saying, 'The severest fighting of the war was followed by the most appalling sights upon the battle-field. Never, I believe, was the ground strewn with the bodies of the dead and the dying in greater numbers or in more shocking attitudes.' General McClellan had been appointed by Lincoln to march into western Maryland and engage Lee there. Lee made his stand at Sharpsburg, a town on Antietam Creek, and McClellan attacked on 17 September 1862. At the close of the battle nearly 23,000 men had been killed or wounded. The two sides had fought themselves to a standstill without a definite result, but on the night of 18 September Lee took his army back into Virginia, his invasion plans in ruins.

Casualties during the Civil War were as much due to disease from bad sanitation and diet, and lack of suitable clothes and shelter, as to bullets and shells. John Will Dyer wrote in *Reminiscences, Four Years in the Confederate Army*, 'We had no anaesthetic dressing then, and all wounds were treated with the cold water treatment, which was to thickly bandage the wound and keep continually wet with cold water, till all signs of inflammation disappeared, and the flesh began to show granulation.' Gangrene was burnt out with nitric acid. 'This was very severe and trying on the nerves of the nurse as well as the patient.'

David H. Strother, a former *Harper's* correspondent, who served first with Pope and later with McClellan, said that after the Confederate retreat he found the dead bodies of the soldiers. 'Many were so covered with dust, torn, crushed and trampled that they resembled clods of earth and you were obliged to look twice before recognizing them as human beings' (*Harper's Magazine*, Vol. XXXVI, February 1868). The wounded were tended in barns and temporary hospitals and those who were not dead were 'strangely hilarious and recklessly at their ease' and 'ready to renew the conflict' (*Harper's Monthly*, XXXVI, 1868).

Wounded escaping from the burning woods of the Wilderness —

ALFRED R. WAUD

'Army of the Potomac : our wounded escaping from the fires in the Wilderness'
1861–5 AMERICAN CIVIL WAR
Original drawing
Pencil and chinese white
Library of Congress

The Wilderness, an area of pine and oak thickets where there had been fighting around Chancellorsville in May 1863, was now the scene of another action when Grant and Lee met for one of the fiercest battles of the war. Grant was now General-in-Chief of all the Federal armies, and the attack launched in the Wilderness in May 1864 was his final assault against the Confederates.

Describing the terrain, *Harper's Weekly* wrote, 'The ground was rolling and covered with dense thickets of dwarf pines and chaparral, so that artillery would have to be dispensed with on either side.' The country was 'almost impenetrable', and the armies fought in near darkness and blindly. After two days fires

started. Waud said that they were 'caused by the explosion of shells, and the fires made for cooking, spreading around. . . . It is not supposed that many lives were lost in this horrible manner; but there were some poor fellows, whose wounds had disabled them, who perished in that dreadful flame. Some were carried off by the ambulance corps, others in blankets suspended to four muskets, and more by the aid of sticks, muskets, or even by crawling. The fire advanced on all sides through the tall grass, and, taking the dry pines, raged up to their top' (*Harper's Weekly*, 24 May 1864).

For Lee the battle was costly, but for the time being Grant's advance had been checked. An engraving of Waud's sketch was published in *Harper's* on 4 June 1864.

ALFRED R. WAUD

'Fruitless attempt of the Army of the Potomac to move toward Rappahannock on 20 January 1863'

1861–5 AMERICAN CIVIL WAR
Original drawing
Pencil, wash and chinese white
Library of Congress

In November 1862, General Burnside replaced McClellan as commander of the Army of the Potomac. He advanced rapidly towards Fredericksburg with the object of crossing the Rappahannock and going on to Richmond. As the pontoon bridges he had ordered had not yet arrived, he delayed at the Rappahannock allowing Lee time to get his army into position. Burnside attacked on 13 December but casualties compelled him to withdraw across the river. His intention was to move upstream and recross beyond Lee's left flank, but rain had churned up the river approaches into impassable mud, in which men and machines floundered.

Harper's published a wood engraving of Waud's drawing, together with a written description, on 14 February 1863: 'The roads under the influence of the rain were becoming shocking; and by daylight, when the boats should all have been on the banks, ready to slide down into the water' only fifteen had arrived. 'The night's rain had made deplorable havoc with the roads. . . . The sand makes the soil pliable, the clay makes it sticky, and the two together form a road out of which, when it rains, the bottom drops, but which is at the same time so tenacious that extrication from its clutch is all but impossible.' While the Federals were ignominiously stuck in the mud, Rebel pickets shouted that they would come over to help them. 'One might fancy some new geological cataclysm had o'ertaken the world; and that he saw around him the elemental wrecks left by another Deluge.' There was an 'indescribable chaos' of pontoons, wagons, artillery on the roads to the river. 'Horses and mules dropped down dead, exhausted with the effort to move their loads through the hideous medium.'

7th N.Y. Heavy Arty. in Barlows charge, in Cold Harbor
Friday June 3rd 1864.

ALFRED R. WAUD

'General Grant's Great Campaign : General Barlow charging the enemy at Cold Harbor, 1 June 1864'

1861–5 AMERICAN CIVIL WAR

Original drawing

Pencil

Library of Congress

By 1 June 1864 the Army of the Potomac under Grant had reached Cold Harbor, near the Chickahominy River and close to Richmond. Grant mounted a massive attack on Lee's defences. General Gibbons's division was followed in the attack by Hancock's 2nd division under Frank Barlow looking 'like a highly independent mounted newsboy . . . attired in a flannel checked shirt; a threadbare pair of trousers, and an old blue kepi' (Horace Porter, *Campaigning with General Grant*).

Barlow's brigade gained a foothold in Lee's lines and Waud's sketch shows the 7th New York Heavy Artillery at the moment of success. *Harper's* describes how 'they got over and into the enemy's parapet, capturing his guns (four light 12 pounders), his colors, and five or six hundred prisoners, about three hundred of whom were secured by promptly passing them to the rear'.

Waud writes, 'This sketch represents a portion of the line at the time when they had captured the first line of rifle-pits, and were about to advance upon the second. The regiment is the New York Seventh Heavy Artillery. Some men are seen over the embankment endeavouring to turn the enemy's captured guns upon them, under the direction of Lieutenant-Colonel Morris, Colonel Porter having been killed in the charge.' Prisoners are being disarmed in the foreground. Near by some soldiers move the dead Colonel in a blanket 'and above a captured flag, with the Virginia State arms emblazoned upon it, is carried by one of our soldiers' (25 June 1864).

When Confederate reinforcements arrived, Barlow's Brigade was forced to retreat. 'It was not merely the overwhelming front that came pressing down upon them . . . but the position they had gained placed them in advance of the whole line of battle, and gave the rebel artillery the opportunity for deadly enfilading fire.' Grant's advance was temporarily checked and there were heavy casualties. Waud's drawing, probably compiled from verbal reports, was good propaganda for a Union battle which had in fact been unsuccessful.

ALFRED R. WAUD
*'General Grant's Campaign: in the trenches
before Petersburg. Sharpshooter 18th Corps'*
1861 AMERICAN CIVIL WAR
Original drawing
Pencil and chinese white
Library of Congress

Petersburg was the Confederate last line of
defence before Richmond. The town held out
under siege through 1864 and 1865. 'It was hell
itself and it is wondrous to me that so many of us
survived the event,' wrote a Pennsylvanian
corporal. 'The over-taxing of the men in
building rifle pits, batteries, forts and cover
ways, in addition to the continuous
sharpshooting; the evening and morning duels,
which were so deadly in our front, being from
one or two hundred yards apart and right in
front of the city, was simply awful. One-half of
the line would fire while the other worked on the
pits or tried to sleep' (G. W. Ward, *History of the
2nd Pennsylvanian Veteran Heavy Artillery*).
Sharpshooters were disliked by both sides and

caused a steady stream of casualties. Firing
always stopped at sunset and sharpshooters
would crawl out and walk about in the night air.
At sunrise everyone was back in position again.

After the war Waud continued to work for
Harper's, and toured the South and West for the
journal in 1866. He contributed illustrations to a
book called *Picturesque America* in 1872, and to
Battles and Leaders of the Civil War in 1887. The
English correspondent G. A. Sala has left a
description of Waud in his heyday as a 'special'
at the camp of the Army of the Potomac in 1863.
He was 'blue-eyed, fair-bearded, strapping and
stalwart, full of loud, cheery laughs and comic
songs, armed to the teeth, jack-booted,
gauntleted, slouch-hatted. . . . He probably knew
more about the several campaigns, the rights and
wrongs of the several fights, the merits and
demerits of the commanders, than two out of
three wearers of generals' shoulder straps. But he
was a prudent man, who could keep his own
counsel, and went on sketching' (*My Diary in
America in the Midst of War*).

WILLIAM WAUD (d. 1878)

'Army of the James: signalling by torches across the James River from General Butler's headquarters'

1861–5 AMERICAN CIVIL WAR
Original drawing
Pencil and wash
Library of Congress

Al Waud's brother William contributed to *Frank Leslie's Illustrated Newspaper* during the first two years of the Civil War, but in 1864 he became a 'special' for *Harper's*. This illustration was completed at General Butler's headquarters on the James River and published as a wood engraving in *Harper's* on 12 November 1864. While Grant was advancing overland towards Richmond, General Butler's army had been sent by water to land on the James River below the Confederate capital. The General devised a way of sending messages across the river by means of signal towers from which flags were used by day and torches by night. 'The messages from the high signal-tower on the other side of the river are read by the sergeant or officer at the telescope, and the reply is signalled by the man with the torch.' Nearby Butler had erected an observation post. The General aimed at clearing a way for Federal gunboats to reduce Richmond's James River defences, but he was thoroughly inept and his schemes were unsuccessful.

There are few personal details available about William Waud, but his obituary in *Harper's* (30 November 1878) mentions that he was an excellent artist, a gifted writer and also an architect who, before leaving for America, had been assistant to Sir Joseph Paxton during the construction of the Crystal Palace.

Charge of Union troops of the left flank of Army Commanded by Genl Stonewall Jackson at Cedar Mountain
Augt 9th 186

EDWIN FORBES (1839–95)
'Nathaniel Banks hits Jackson's left flank at Cedar Mountain', 9 August 1862
1861–5 AMERICAN CIVIL WAR
Original drawing
Pencil
Library of Congress

In 1861 Edwin Forbes was commissioned as staff artist for *Frank Leslie's Illustrated Newspaper* to report on the progress of the Army of the Potomac. He followed the Union armies from Manassas in 1862 until the siege of Petersburg in 1864, often covering the same ground as Al Waud of *Harper's*. He made quick sketches on the battlefield, refining them later, and always made copious notes for the wood engraver. His work included some stirring battle sketches, but he was as much interested in scenes of camp life.

In 1862 Pope was in command of the Federal troops in northern Virginia. On 9 August Stonewall Jackson attacked his camp at Cedar Mountain and drove the Union forces back. Forbes's drawing was accompanied by a written account in *Leslie's*: 'At three o'clock skirmishing commenced. The cavalry again rode forward and were immediately fired on. The enemy opened with the battery in front of the house and clump of trees' in the sketch. After a few minutes General Geary's brigade filed out of the woods in the rear, followed by the brigades of Generals Prince, Green and Gordon. Geary's brigade took up their position in a cornfield on the right. Prince's brigade was in front of Knapp's battery and Crawford's in the wheatfield also on the right, 'across which he charged and lost a great part of his command'.

After the bombardment had been going on for some time, Generals Geary and Crawford attacked the two Confederate batteries, one of which was in position near the white farmhouse, and the other in the corner by the woods. 'Our boys fought like heroes or devils; and although met by an immense force of the enemy, they succeeded in driving him back through one piece of woods into the open field beyond. The fighting in this wood was most terrible; men fought bayonet to bayonet' (30 August 1862). When Pope withdrew to the Rappahannock, Virginian negro slaves followed his army.

EDWIN FORBES

'*Charge of the 9th New York Zouaves on the right flank of the rebel army, Antietam, 3.30 pm, 17 September 1862*'
1861–5 AMERICAN CIVIL WAR
Original drawing
Pencil
Library of Congress

The terrible scenes at the Battle of Antietam in September 1862 affected all the correspondents who were there. Al Waud sent eloquent despatches and drawings to *Harper's* and Forbes did the same for *Leslie's*.

The incident illustrated in Forbes's sketch occurred in the afternoon of 17 September. The artist shows the beautiful countryside in which the fighting took place. He describes in *Leslie's* how Hawkins's Zouaves 'found the enemy ready drawn up under cover of the hills, and advanced in line of battle on the enemy's new position, about half a mile distant. The ground over which they advanced was open clover and ploughed fields, the latter very difficult and fatiguing to march in, owing to the softness of the ground.

The enemy's guns, fourteen in number, kept up a terrible fire on our advancing line, which never wavered, but slowly toiled along, receiving shelter, however, when they were in the hollows. They were halted for a few moments to rest in the hollow nearest the enemy's position, and then were ordered to charge with a yell. As they came up the hill in front of the enemy's batteries, they received a heavy volley from a large force of infantry behind a stone wall about 200 feet in front of the enemy's batteries. Our men, though terribly decimated, gave them a volley in return, and then went on with the bayonet. The enemy did not stay to contest the ground, and . . . broke and ran, leaving their guns' (11 October 1862).

The *Daily Telegraph* correspondent G. A. Sala, who described the Zouaves shortly after this incident, did not find them so impressive: 'The uniform is a pretty close copy of the picturesque Oriental garb, the donning of which had turned so many "gamins de Paris" into dashing soldiers; but the American Zouaves are miserably shabby' (*My Diary in America in the Midst of War*).

EDWIN FORBES

'Grant's army cheer his decision to continue the march southwards in spite of the defeat in the Wilderness', 7 May 1864

1861–5 AMERICAN CIVIL WAR

Original drawing

Pencil

Library of Congress

Grant was appointed supreme commander of the Union land forces by Lincoln in March 1864 and at the beginning of May he launched new offensives against Atlanta and Richmond. The Army of the Potomac crossed the Rapidan on 4 May, but instead of pressing on immediately to Spottsylvania, their first objective, Grant ordered the men to camp for the night in the Wilderness area to await the arrival of supply trains. Lee knew that it was to his advantage to engage Grant's army in the awkward thickets of the Wilderness.

As General Porter wrote in his memoirs, 'The outlook was limited in all directions by the almost impenetrable forest with its interlacing trees and tangled undergrowth. . . . The locality is well described by its name. It was a wilderness in the most forbidding sense of the word.' (*Campaigning with Grant*). The Confederates were familiar with the country, and their tactics better adapted to fighting there. The battle raged from 4 May until 6 May.

At one point it looked as if Grant's own safety was in jeopardy. 'Warren's troops were driven back on a portion of his line in front of general headquarters, stragglers were making their way to the rear, the enemy's shells were beginning to fall on the knoll where General Grant was seated on the stump of a tree, and it looked for a while as if the tide of battle would sweep over that point of the field.' General Porter was glad to see that Grant remained cool and soon the position was no longer in immediate danger of being overrun. By the evening of 6 May the woods caught fire and made the continuation of fighting impossible. The moment shown in Forbes's drawing may have been imaginary and drawn for propaganda reasons. In spite of casualties, on 7 May Grant decided that the advance towards Richmond should continue, and his army moved on to Spottsylvania.

Lw. U S Grant at Wilderness May 7th 1864.

EDWIN FORBES
'Home Sweet Home'
1861–5 AMERICAN CIVIL WAR
Original drawing
Pencil and chinese white
Library of Congress

In 1876 Forbes published *Life Studies of the Great Army*, a series of etchings based on drawings made during the war. This picture may have originated in a sketch made during the winter of 1862–3 when the Army of the Potomac was at Falmouth, Virginia. The men lived in a variety of accommodation. The wagoners' huts were the grandest as they had transport to carry window frames and other housebuilding equipment. Most of the men were in mud huts or tents, while picket huts were generally constructed of pine boughs thrown hastily together.

This hut has a foundation of logs, plastered with clay and topped by a tent. The chimney pot is a ploughshare. It housed two men and contained a bed made of pine boughs in the back. The weather was cold during the winter and the men had to forage for fuel. This hut had a sod fireplace and the hut interior was probably lined with sods for extra warmth. Candles stuck on the ends of bayonets provided light, or sometimes an improvised lamp was made with a sardine tin filled with grease and a lighted rag floating on the top for a wick. One man in the picture is playing a homemade violin.

The troops of both sides did their best to make themselves comfortable in camp and looted food and equipment to make up for the deficiencies of the Commissariat. G. A. Sala, who visited the Union camp at this time, fastidiously found them a 'dirty lot'.

EDWIN FORBES
'The newspaper correspondent'
1861–5 AMERICAN CIVIL WAR
Original drawing
Pencil and chinese white
Library of Congress

Another of Forbes's drawings published as an etching after the war, this picture gives a glamorized image of an intrepid newspaper correspondent riding to be first with the news. Forbes enjoyed drawing equestrian subjects but unfortunately used the current artistic convention for showing a galloping horse. All four of the animal's feet are off the ground at once, its nostrils flare and its eyeballs protrude. It was not until the end of the century that experiments with slow motion photography demonstrated to artists the correct movement of a horse's legs.

News was vitally important for soldiers of both sides during the war. G. A. Sala noticed that 'the consumption of journalism in the Federal armies is tremendous, and the perusal of newspapers appears to yield the men unceasing and unfailing delight' (*My Diary in America in the Midst of War*). Newspaper sellers dashed to the camps on horseback and papers vied with each other to see who could get the news to the army first.

The sketches Forbes made at the Civil War were the basis of his work for the rest of his life. In 1876 he was awarded a medal at the Philadelphia Centennial for *Life Studies of the Great Army*. In later years he worked on illustrated histories of war for children and, in 1890, published *An Artist's Story of the Great War*.

An actual sketch, made on the spot by one of the Special Artists of Frank Leslie's Illustrated Newspaper.

Mr. Leslie holds the copyright and reserves the exclusive right of publication.

HENRI LOVIE
'Death of Lyons', 10 August 1861
1861–5 AMERICAN CIVIL WAR
Original drawing
Pencil
New York Public Library

Henri Lovie was a special artist for *Frank Leslie's Illustrated Newspaper* and in June 1861 obtained a pass to join the Federal expeditionary force going up the Missouri River. Captain Nathaniel Lyons had been in action at St Louis in May where he had disarmed the state militia and fired on a crowd of civilians in an attempt to prevent Missouri seceding from the Union. Now a brigadier general, Lyons led his division on to Jefferson City on 14 June and then to Boonville, which was the headquarters of the Missouri state militia. The town was taken on 16 June after a short fight, which was watched by the correspondents from their ship. When Lovie and his colleagues finally went on shore they were almost shot by Lyons's men who thought that they were Rebel scouts. Lovie later said that he had 'no objections to running reasonable risks from the enemy, but to be killed by mistake would be damned unpleasant' (*Cincinnati Daily Gazette*, 29 June 1861).

Lyons was killed at the Battle of Wilson's Creek on 10 August when his troops were outnumbered by Sterling Price's Missouri state force. Two of Lyons's best regiments were beaten back under the Rebel attack and Lyons was wounded, and his horse shot from under him. His aide gave him another mount, and as he was rallying his men for a final charge he received the fatal bullet wound. Fighting continued for two more hours before the Federals retreated, taking Lyons's body back to Springfield. Correspondents were told that they had to manage for themselves in the retreat, and many tore up their work thinking that they might be shot as spies if caught. Lovie refused to abandon his sketches and was able to escape to Lebanon (Kentucky). From there he went on to report the news from Rolla in Missouri. *Leslie's* provided its correspondents with a special sketch pad, and their copyright notice can be seen in the bottom left-hand corner. An engraving of this picture appeared in *Leslie's* on 31 August 1861.

The Battle of Munfordville — Sunday
the Rebels charge through the abatis in front
of fortifications

N.B. Put as much fallen timber and dead li_
between the figures as you can —

AN actual sketch, made on the spot by
of the Special Artists of Frank Leslie's Illustrated Newspaper.
Mr Leslie holds the copyright and
serves the exclusive right of publication.

HENRI LOVIE
*'Battle of Munfordville, Kentucky, 14
September 1862. Rebels charge through the
abatis in front of the fortifications'*
1861–5 AMERICAN CIVIL WAR
Original drawing
Pencil
New York Public Library

The Confederate army under Braxton Bragg
moved north into Kentucky during August 1862,
hoping to win the state over for the Union.
Crossing the Cumberland River they attacked
Buell's Army of the Ohio at Munfordville.
Lovie's sketch shows the 10th Mississippi
Regiment, commanded by Colonel R. A. Smith,
under Union fire. The official report of the
action states that Smith, 'being entirely ignorant
of the ground to be passed over, came within
range of the enemy's guns from the right of their
works and in front of the abatis of fallen trees, in

a position where it was equally dangerous to
advance or retreat, and immediately advanced
against the works.' Smith was wounded and the
attack failed but Bragg sent in a supporting force
and the Union commander surrendered on 17
September. One of Lovie's notes to the engraver
reads: 'Put as much fallen timber and dead limbs
between the figures as you can.' The engraving
was published in *Leslie's* on 25 October 1862.

HENRI LOVIE
'Death of Colonel Garesche, at the battle of Stones River, 31 December 1862'
1861–5 AMERICAN CIVIL WAR
Original drawing
Pencil
New York Public Library

Soon after the Battle of Munfordville, William S. Rosencrans replaced Buell as Union commander, and in December 1862 was in action against Bragg at Stones River. Fighting commenced on the 30th and lasted for three days, the Confederates being at last forced to withdraw to the south-west. Casualties on both sides were severe and Rosencrans did not press home the attack. In the sketch Rosencrans is third from the left, with his Chief of Staff Colonel Garesche on his left at the moment of his decapitation by a cannon ball. Major Skinner is on the far side of him. Other casualties from the same cannon ball are in the foreground. The background is sketched in faintly with a note saying 'the 4 cedar trees a feature!'

Little is known about Lovie's personal history. Before the war he was connected with the engraving firms Lovie and Bauerle, and Lovie, Bauerle and Bruen in Cincinnati, and was active as a portrait and landscape painter. He may have returned to Cincinnati once the war was over.

WINSLOW HOMER (1836–1910)
'Wounded soldier being given a drink from a canteen'
1861–5 AMERICAN CIVIL WAR
Original drawing
Charcoal and white chalk on green paper
Cooper-Hewitt Collection, Smithsonian Institution

Winslow Homer began his career as a black and white artist, lithographer and illustrator. It was not until he reached the age of twenty-seven that he also began to paint in oils and watercolours. He started working for *Harper's Weekly* when he was twenty-one, and had a short spell at the front during the Civil War representing the journal. He saw action at Yorktown and Fair Oaks, returning after Malvern Hill. After this he paid one or two other short visits to the front, but he was not a regular war 'special'. Most of his sketches of the war were in fact completed in New York and he may have drawn some of them direct on to the wooden block for publication in *Harper's*. Like Edwin Forbes, Homer enjoyed

illustrating everyday scenes of camp life. Apart from working for *Harper's* during the war, he also completed a series of lithographs entitled *Campaign Sketches* in 1863. He followed this up with some souvenir cards, each showing Federal troops at war. When the war was over he continued as a free-lance illustrator and in 1866 went to Paris to study art. In later life he became an illustrator of the American scene and country life. After 1874 he gave up black and white illustration and concentrated on painting.

THEODORE R. DAVIS (1840–94)

'The Vigilance committee at Memphis, Tennessee, robbing our special artist of his sketches'

1861–5 AMERICAN CIVIL WAR
Wood engraving
Harper's Weekly, 22 June 1861, p. 394 top

Theodore Davis joined *Harper's* in March 1861 and made his first trip for the journal to the Southern states just before the beginning of the war. He claimed that he accompanied William Russell, *The Times* correspondent, but Russell did not deign to mention him in *My Diary North and South*. Davis was one of the most important of the *Harper's* artists during the war, second only to Al Waud. He saw the capture of Port Royal, the battle between the *Monitor* and *Merrimac*, the fighting at Shiloh, the capture of Corinth, Antietam, the surrender of Vicksburg, the Battle of Chattanooga, the Atlanta campaign and the Grand March to the sea. Although he was twice wounded, he considered his trip to the South in 1861, where this sketch was made, to have been one of the most dangerous journeys he had ever undertaken.

The unpleasant adventure in the picture occurred on his return from New Orleans when the Memphis Vigilance Committee enquired 'who he was, where he came from, what he was doing' and then went through his luggage. They examined his sketches minutely, each member pocketing two or three of the best, and 'as the only revenge Mr Davis could take on these polite highway robbers, he sketched them in the act of despoiling him'. After the war *Harper's* sent Davis with Waud to the South to show the results of the war and 'the rising of a new world from chaos' (*Harper's Weekly*, 28 April 1866).

THEODORE R. DAVIS

'Discovering the remains of Lieutenant Kidder and ten men of the Seventh United States Cavalry'

1867–91 INDIAN WARS
Wood engraving
Harper's Weekly, 17 August 1867, p. 513 bottom

Davis first travelled to the Western states of America in 1865 to report on conditions there for *Harper's*. At Smoky Hill Spring a band of Indians attacked the coach in which he was travelling, and he 'picked up his rifle and rent its contents at the most gaudily gotten up Indian' of the party and helped to beat them off. In April 1867 he joined General Hancock's expedition to Kansas and Nebraska, and witnessed several more skirmishes with Indians. Custer had joined Hancock's command and *Harper's* reported that their 'special' had been 'for the last six months . . . roving the plains with General Custer after the Indians', wearing a specially designed 'plains costume' (7 September 1867).

On 3 August *Harper's* reported an attack by a party of Sioux under 'Pawnee Killer'. The Indian chief asked Custer to meet him in conference. 'The Indians then asked for sugar, coffee, etc, and ammunition – and this, too, while scalp-locks of fair Anglo-Saxon hair were hanging to their clothing by way of ornament.' Shortly afterwards, at Beaver Creek, Custer's party found the corpses of Lieutenant Kidder and his men. The Lieutenant had only recently come to Fort Sedgwick and had been ordered to deliver important despatches from General Sherman to Custer. Kidder missed the route and the party was surrounded by several hundred Indians, who drove them into a ravine and killed them. 'The remains were too horribly mutilated to enable the officers to recognize any of the party.' They were buried near the spot where they fell.

After his return to New York Davis continued to illustrate Western subjects for *Harper's*. His regular contributions to the journal ceased about 1884 when he became a free-lance.

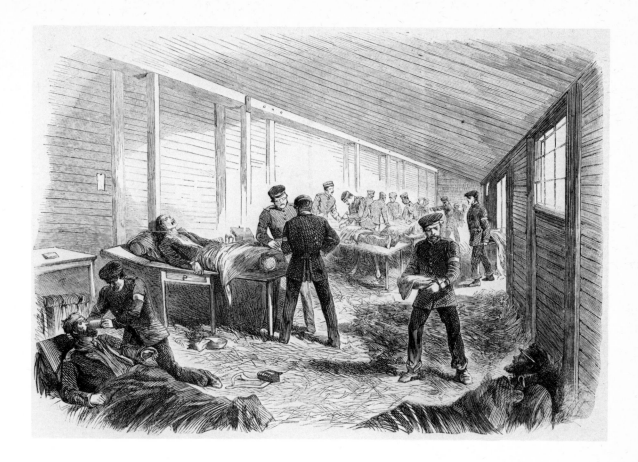

ROBERT THOMAS LANDELLS
(1833–77)
'Temporary field hospital behind the second Prussian Parallel at Düppel : scene in the amputating hut'
1864 GERMAN–DANISH WAR
Wood engraving
Illustrated London News, 7 May 1864, p. 444 bottom

Robert Landells was the son of Ebenezer Landells, a pupil of the engraver Thomas Bewick, and worked as an artist for *Punch* and the *Illustrated London News* in the early days of the journals. He was a 'special' for the *Illustrated London News* at the Crimean War and covered the Prussian side in the German–Danish War of 1863, which 'gave occasion for Mr R. T. Landells to exert his special talent in delineating various incidents of military life, and the figures and movements of soldiery' (*Illustrated London News* Obituary, 1877). Later he became an expert in Prussian affairs, joining their forces for the Prussian–Austrian War of 1866 and the Franco–Prussian War of 1870–1.

He was a childhood hero for Irving Montagu,

who remembered that he had 'pictured Bob in top-boots and spurs riding round the lines making graphic sketches in a very hot-bed of shot and shell' (*Wanderings of a War Artist*). He was popular among other correspondents, and Archibald Forbes, the *Daily News* correspondent, recollected in 1890 how 'I have spliced the mainbrace and dealt in horseflesh with handsome, sweet natured Tom Landells . . .' (*Graphic*, 6 December 1890). He was also a cultivated man whose paintings were popular with Queen Victoria, and who was accepted in society in Britain and abroad.

During the German–Danish War the *Illustrated London News* was on the side of the Danes in this 'cruel and unprovoked war'. On 18 April the Prussians finally stormed the forts at Düppel, 'the Danes being greatly overmatched'. There were severe casualties and another picture in the same issue of the *Illustrated London News* shows the Crown Prince of Prussia and his companions watching the dead being collected as they look on 'the bloody work of the morning, triumphant in the pride of military power.'

ROBERT THOMAS LANDELLS
'A balloon from Paris passing over Versailles'
1870–1 FRANCO–PRUSSIAN WAR
Wood engraving
Illustrated London News, 22 October 1870, p. 420

Having the advantage of speaking German and knowing the Crown Prince of Prussia personally, Landells joined the Prussian headquarters at Versailles in the autumn of 1870 during the Franco–Prussian War. He was with the Prussians throughout the siege, celebrating the Christmas of 1870 in typical German style with plumcake, punch and a Christmas tree outside the starving city of Paris.

This engraving from a sketch by Landells shows a balloon from the besieged city passing over Versailles. Balloons were becoming an emblem of Parisian resistance. A number of them, which had been found left over from the Great Exhibition of 1867, were patched up and used. They were made of varnished cotton and filled with highly explosive coal gas.

On 15 October the *Illustrated London News* recorded, 'Balloons are daily sent off from Paris, and are carried by the prevailing winds to the provinces which are unoccupied by the Germans. They are followed by Prussian light cavalry as long as they continue in sight.' A regular 'balloon post' was established by M. Ramport, Minister of Posts and many of the illustrations and despatches appearing in the *Illustrated London News* at this time have 'By balloon post' written beside them. The Prussians began to take counter-measures and the Parisians were forced to send up the balloons by night. This sometimes had unexpected results, and one balloon *Ville d'Orleans* landed, to its crew's surprise, in Norway, after a flight of fifteen hours.

After the war was over Landells was given the Prussian Iron Cross for 'his exertions to aid in the relief of the sick and wounded soldiers in the winter campaign on the Loire.' He did not act as a war correspondent again, but concentrated on his painting career at home.

SYDNEY PRIOR HALL (1842–1922)
'Arrest of our artist at Nancy'
1870–1 FRANCO–PRUSSIAN WAR
Wood engraving
Graphic, 6 August 1870, p. 140 left

Sydney Hall was the son of Harry Hall, a painter of sporting life. He studied at the Royal Academy and had a reputation as an artist before being taken on as an illustrator by the new British picture paper, the *Graphic*. His only campaign as war correspondent was the Franco–Prussian War.

In August 1870 soon after his arrival in France he reported that, 'Artists and Special Correspondents are having a hard time of it at the seat of war just now; a sketch-book is an object of suspicion, and inquiries even of the most general character are sufficient to consign a man to the guard house for the night.' He was arrested three times by the French at Nancy in August and, on the occasion illustrated, he and his companions had some difficulty in proving their innocence. Although released in the end

their accusers were 'by no means satisfied with the decision, and showed signs of the most decided hostility.'

In September it was the turn of the Prussians to arrest Hall. The *Graphic* reported on 10 September that he had been 'most courteously treated by his captors, and, being now released, follows the Prussian army with his sketch book and pencil, and has, we hope, passed through his last arrest.' In fact he was in trouble again almost immediately when he tried to get to Strasbourg with a Yorkshire doctor. The two men were marched back to Holsheim under escort. 'On our way back under guard I trudged along with chin on chest, very downcast at such treatment, but the doctor was jovial.' Many of the other correspondents suffered in the same way. Irving Montagu recalled that during the spy fever one correspondent, 'when required to show his papers, having no passport to produce, handed up his tailor's bill which he happened to have in his pocket, an awe-inspiring document . . .' (*Wanderings of a War Artist*).

SYDNEY PRIOR HALL
'Shaving the enemy at Montmirail'
1870–1 FRANCO–PRUSSIAN WAR
Wood engraving
Graphic, 8 October 1870, p. 353 bottom

Harry Furniss, the caricaturist, recalled in his memoirs that Sydney Hall was considered to be the best artist among the 'specials' of the period. 'Up to his day, and in fact after it, special artists were little more than special correspondents. . . . Hall struck a new line by giving human incidents of the picturesque side of war' (*My Bohemian Days*). It is difficult to judge his skill from the engravings made by the *Graphic* from his sketches. A clearer idea of his work at the Franco–Prussian War can be obtained from his own book, *Sketches From an Artist's Portfolio*, which was published in 1875.

The incident in this illustration shows 'the enemy in the person of a German soldier . . . being operated upon by a female barber.' The English have 'a natural objection to being taken by the nose by women; but this German, who is doubtless an advocate for women's rights, seems to be above such petty prejudices.' The barber's shop is primitive; 'a nest of pigeon holes contains the towels of the establishment's frequentiers; the shampooing apparatus is simple in the extreme', and spectators can watch proceedings through the window. 'If there were 100,000 Prussians,' said an old Frenchman on seeing Hall's sketch, 'and 100,000 perruquiers, the war would soon be finished,' and illustrated his words 'by an expressive pass across his throat.'

SYDNEY PRIOR HALL
'Once more in the sun'
1870–1 FRANCO–PRUSSIAN WAR
Wood engraving
Graphic, 26 November 1870, p. 509

Hall arrived at the outskirts of Paris with the Prussian army at the end of October 1870. He bought a horse and christened it 'Graphy' in honour of the journal. He found the days at Versailles tedious and wrote, 'I confess I have made these sketches for want of something better to do. There are days in the long monotony of a siege when even a special artist must be idle' (*Sketches from an Artist's Portfolio*).

The palace of Versailles was made into a hospital for wounded German soldiers. 'They recover quicker in a tent hospital, they say, because the wind can blow through it and round it, and the principle is recognised in our permanent hospitals, where the plan now is to build them in separate blocks.' When the sun came out 'those patients who were on the road to recovery were wrapped up in an extra blanket, and borne out upon the sunny terrace, there in the fresh air to eat their dinners with wonderful appetite for sick men.' The men in the illustration are officers and each has a servant in attendance, and a sister to superintend. Their comrades drop in for a chat. The man sitting at the foot of one of the beds is Mr Home, the spiritualist, 'the counseller of Princes and the bugbear of Priests.' When the men were stronger they were taken by van to Nanteuil and on to Prussia.

After the war Hall remained with the *Graphic* as an illustrator and became known for his pictures of Royal tours and Court ceremonial. He also toured the American West for the journal. Archibald Forbes paid tribute to his work in 1890 saying, 'That remarkable series of highly finished full-page campaign pictures which Sydney Hall sent to the *Graphic* in 1870–1 can never cease to be remembered by anyone who saw them.'

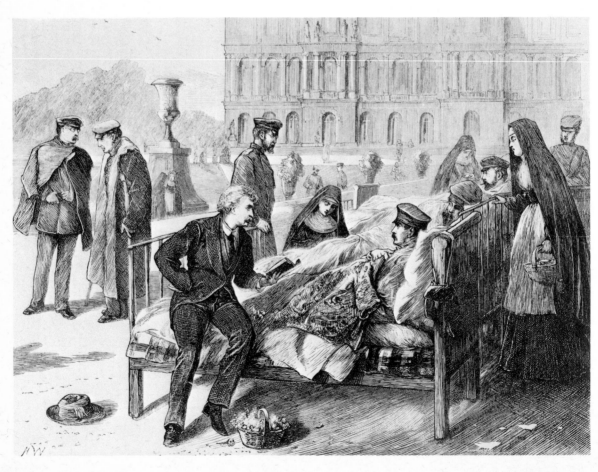

JULES PELCOQ
'Wounded from the ramparts landed at the Quai de la Megisserie, Paris'
1870–1 FRANCO–PRUSSIAN WAR
Wood engraving from drawing sent by 'balloon post'
Illustrated London News, 21 January 1871, p. 64–5

A Parisian book illustrator, Jules Pelcoq, was a correspondent on the French side for the *Illustrated London News* at the Franco–Prussian War. He was shut up in Paris throughout the siege and had to despatch his work by balloon to London. The incident in the picture took place in November 1870, when the city's troops made a desperate attempt to break through the surrounding Prussian army. The 'Great Sortie' was to consist of a triple attack on the German lines. It was difficult for journalists to find out how the attack was going, but they realized that it had not been successful when they saw the wounded streaming back. They were brought by water in one of the small river steamers 'that ply on the Seine, under the charge of the Ambulance or Field-Hospital Society.' They were then put on hand-litters and transferred to vans and carts for the military hospitals in the town. 'The red-cross standard above the tent erected upon the landing-stage, with the same emblem displayed over the vans and waggons, proclaims the lamentable business in hand.' It is evening, and the work is being carried on by torchlight, 'the bracardiers of the National Guards labouring, with the utmost diligence and care, to assist in speedily placing their unfortunate brothers in arms. . . . There are some of those more slightly wounded, who have carried off such trophies as Prussian spiked helmets or needle guns, which they show to admiring friends.' The wounded's troubles were not over when they reached the base hospitals as the chances of them dying from septicaemia or gangrene were high.

JULES PELCOQ
'Killing an elephant for food in the Jardin des Plantes, Paris'

1870–1 FRANCO–PRUSSIAN WAR

Wood engraving from drawing sent by 'balloon post'
Illustrated London News, 28 January 1871, p. 77

Although not positively identified as being by Jules Pelcoq, this engraving is almost certainly based on a sketch or report sent in by him. During the siege hunger was feared more than the Prussian bombardment. At length 'it was found advisable to order the killing of the wild beasts and birds in the zoological collection.' This measure was as much to avoid feeding them as for a food supply. Six or seven hundred horses were slaughtered every day, 'dog's flesh was worth two francs the pound', cats and rats were part of the diet, so it 'was not to be doubted that dainty pickings would be found in the Parisian Zoo.' Leading restaurants served kangaroos, bears, deer and antelopes. *The Times* correspondent reported a dinner 'where one of the dishes was a few slices of elephant's trunk, often described by African hunters as a very choice morsel.' The cost of a slice was about £1.4s, 'the flesh very tender, and not badly flavoured.'

In December, Castor and Pollux, two young elephants in the Jardin d'Acclimation were killed, with lamentations from the Press, who described their death agonies. The animals were sold to Deboos, the proprietor of the Boucherie Anglaise on Boulevard Haussmann and no doubt were quickly bought up by the starving rich of Paris.

CHAM (ARNADEE CHARLES HENRI, COUNT OF NOË) (1819–79)
'Queueing for rat meat'
1870–1 FRANCO–PRUSSIAN WAR
Lithograph
Le Charivari, 8 December 1870
Victoria and Albert Museum

Another view on the food shortage in Paris during the siege is provided by Cham's caricature from the French illustrated paper *Le Charivari*. During the freezing winter of 1870–1, rat-hunting became a fashionable sport. As the Seine had frozen over, making fishing impossible, the *Paris Journal* gave suggestions on how to 'fish for sewer rats with a hook and line bated with tallow'. Rats were food for a rich man, as elaborate sauces were needed to make them palatable and specialities like '*salmi de rats*' were on the menu of the Jockey Club. Professor Sheppard discovered that 'rats, to my surprise, taste somewhat like birds' (*Shut up in Paris*).

Gradually food vanished from the shops, particularly items like bread and potatoes which had been the staple diet of the poor. All foreign correspondents, whether they had been in Paris during the siege or not, wrote about the strange meals that the inhabitants had been forced to eat. Irving Montagu of the *Illustrated London News*, who only got into Paris after the siege was over, recalled in his autobiography, 'Among the odd dishes on which Paris fed, dog was said to be the most nutritious. They called it saddle of mutton, and sold it from three to five francs a pound.'

While the siege was on, newspapers were much in demand by the inhabitants to combat boredom, and as it was difficult to obtain much news from the outside world, illustrations became more important.

ALBERT ROBIDA (1848–1926)

*'Fighting in Père Lachaise cemetery,
27 May 1871'*

1871 PARIS COMMUNE

Wood engraving, redrawn by Daniel Vierge
Le Monde Illustré, 24 June 1871, p. 385 bottom

The French illustrated papers were similar in
lay-out and content to their British and
American counterparts. *Le Monde Illustré* had
been established in 1857 and Robida was one of
the regular artists. During desperate fighting in
the last days of the Commune, the Communards
were cornered in Père Lachaise cemetery. Two
hundred National Guards and two batteries of
guns defended the position, but the Government
troops under General Vinoy were able to
infiltrate and a terrible battle was fought among
the tombs and gravestones of the cemetery.
Robida's illustration shows the position at
8.00 p.m. on 27 May as Government troops
cleared out the last of the rebels. On the right is
Balzac's tomb and on the left Charles Nodier's.
Irving Montagu, an English correspondent who
went into the cemetery shortly after the fighting
was over, wrote in his autobiography, 'It was a
gruesome sight, was Père la Chaise. Tomb-
stones besmeared with blood, chipped and
broken. . . . The earth was literally churned up
with human blood. . . . Distinctly do I remember
how it rose over the very soles of my boots, and
clogged the cavity between these and the
uppers, just as the mud of every-day life is
wont to do.' Robida worked at one time or
another for most of the French papers as an
illustrator and caricaturist. He was also a
designer and book illustrator and after the First
World War published *Les Villes Martyres*.

DANIEL VIERGE (1851–1904)

'The inhabitants of Neuilly return to Paris by the Porte des Ternes'

1871 PARIS COMMUNE
Wood engraving
Le Monde Illustré, 6 May 1871, p. 284

Daniel Vierge was the son of Vicente Urrabieta Ortiz, a leading Spanish illustrator. He studied at l'Academie des Beaux-Arts of Madrid, his studies being interrupted by the Franco–Prussian war in 1870. He worked as an illustrator for *Le Monde Illustré*, sometimes providing the sketches himself and at other times redrawing other contributors' work for publication. This illustration shows refugees from Neuilly entering Paris during the Commune. After the Paris Commune was proclaimed on 28 March 1871, Government artillery steadily bombarded the suburbs of the city, and the village of Neuilly, which had been untouched during the Prussian attack the previous year, came under fire. On 25 April, Thiers agreed to the Communards' request for evacuation of the inhabitants, as by this time there was hardly a house left standing in the village. Once the people were evacuated the bombardment recommenced. After the war Vierge did some book illustration, including pictures for Victor Hugo's *L'Année Terrible*.

IRVING MONTAGU (c.1843–?)

'The camp of The Times *and* Illustrated London News *correspondents attacked by wolves'*

1877–8 RUSSO–TURKISH WAR
Wood engraving
Illustrated London News, 10 November 1877, p. 441

Irving Montagu was a childhood friend of Robert Landells, and determined to follow in his footsteps as a 'special'. He was in Switzerland when the Franco–Prussian War broke out and persuaded the *Illustrated London News* to employ him as a correspondent. He soon discovered that the quickest way to get to the front line was to join an ambulance, as for an artist 'subjects innumerable abound, besides which one may sometimes be of some small use to those professionally engaged' (*Wanderings of a War Artist*). He was in Paris during the siege, and in 1874 covered the Carlist War, having an alarming experience when some Carlists he was sketching shot the leg of his camp stool from under him. He firmly believed that 'the most hasty sketch taken on the spot' was superior to 'the most elaborate one done from memory', and that a picturesque setting for a battle was 'as effective in its way as the picture itself.'

When covering the Russo–Turkish War, Montagu and *The Times* correspondent, R. Coningsby, disguised themselves as merchants to get to the front line, because the Russians discouraged correspondents. They wore 'huge fur-lined greatcoats and muffin shaped hats' and sold provisions to the troops as a cover. On the way a Turkish shell hit their cart and destroyed Montagu's portmanteau, leaving a mess of 'broken brushes, flannel shirts, smashed pots of Liebig's essence of meat, and broken bottles of Dr Collis Browne's chlorodyn.' Wolves attacked their camp outside Plevna. According to Coningsby's report, he scared away the wolves by brandishing 'a sketch by the special artist of the *Illustrated London News*'. The effect was magical and 'with a howl that I can never forget they frantically tore away, far far out into their dreary Balkan retreat.' When some of the beasts returned Montagu retaliated by reading them a report by Coningsby from *The Times*. At this the wolves gave up and the correspondents could at last get some sleep.

After the war Montagu worked as a reporter on home affairs and completed his war memoirs, which were embellished with anecdotes of this kind.

MELTON PRIOR (1845–1910)

'Sketches from Coomassie: the King's slaughtering place'

1873–4 2ND ASHANTI WAR

Wood engraving

Illustrated London News, 25 April 1874, pp. 388–9

Melton Prior's début as a war artist in 1873 marks the beginning of the golden age of the British war 'special'. Prior was twenty-nine years old and recently married when he was given his first chance by William Ingram of the *Illustrated London News* to cover the Ashanti Campaign. The Ashanti had attacked British trading posts at Elmina and Cape Coast Castle.

Prior arrived on 16 December 1873 and soon found that sketching in the tropics had its drawbacks. 'In the tent the sun strikes through so powerfully as to give you the sensation of working in the hottest room of a Turkish bath.' However by 6.00 p.m. when the sun had gone down, sketching was only possible by the light of 'a bad candle stuck in a champagne bottle.' He was shown the ropes by more experienced correspondents, who included Henry Stanley, the African explorer and correspondent for the *New York Herald*, and George Henty of the *Standard*, later famous as a writer of adventure stories. The expedition was led by Sir Garnet Wolseley who hated all correspondents, and referred to them as 'those newly invented curses to armies, who eat the rations of fighting men and do no work at all' (Wolseley, *The Story of a Soldier's Life*).

The party marched inland to Kumasi, the Ashanti capital and burnt it. Prior, who fought side by side with the soldiers, was forced to kill two warriors with Stanley's rifle. He took part in the looting of the Ashanti palace and was rather disgusted to find that two buckles which he had purloined were 'the commonest Brummagen rubbish' (*Campaigns of a War Correspondent*). He sketched Kumasi as it burned and was probably back in England by the time the engraving of the 'King's slaughtering place' was published. The area, discovered in February, was 'adjoining the city market, where the dead bodies of hundreds of human victims, slaughtered by the atrocious customs of the Ashantee kingdom, are thrown to lie unburied, or to be devoured by panthers, wild dogs, and carnivorous birds.'

MELTON PRIOR

'The correspondents of the Rousski Mir *and the* Illustrated London News *on their way from Risano to Peco Pavlovitch's camp at Piva'*

1875–6 REVOLT IN HERZEGOVINA
Wood engraving
Illustrated London News, 15 January 1876, p. 56

When a revolt in Herzegovina broke out in July 1875, Prior was sent to join the Bulgarian leader Peco Pavlovitch. He had a dramatic journey through snow-covered mountains in the company of the Russian correspondent Pierre de Monteverdi. Prior relates in his memoirs how 'there was no road, but everlasting going up and down amongst rugged rocks, and occasionally jumping from one stone to another; in places the track was almost impassable.' They hired an escort of Herzegovinans for protection, as the area was dangerous. The journey took many days and food was scarce. 'A sardine, a biscuit and a cup of coffee would often constitute our day's meal.' Even the horses got tired and the two correspondents had to finish their journey on foot.

Luckily Monteverdi spoke the language and was able to talk to the Bulgarian leader when they arrived. He presented Peco with a sword on behalf of the Russian people who sympathized with his cause. 'The chief received it with what, no doubt, he meant as thanks, but which I personally thought was a growl,' recorded Prior. The Turks were too strong for the rebels, and burnt villages and slaughtered many of the inhabitants. 'These Turks have no pity, no compassion, no bowels. They have not even the pity of wild beasts,' wrote J. A. MacGahan of the *Daily News*.

In 1877 Russia intervened in support of the Balkan countries, and this time Prior covered the Turkish side. At the Battle of Sinankeu he described to readers of the *Illustrated London News* how he was writing and drawing by the light of a 'naked candle between my feet, which act as a candlestick. I am surrounded by the dead, and the groans of the wounded are most painful to hear.'

MELTON PRIOR
'Arrival of the body of the Prince Imperial at Itelezi Camp'
1879 ZULU WAR
Wood engraving
Illustrated London News, 19 July 1879, p. 57

The causes of the British expedition to Zululand were similar to those leading to the Ashanti War five years earlier, reinforced by the fear that a large, well-trained Zulu army on the Natal border might threaten British colonists there. Prior joined General Newdigate's advance on Ulundi, and he described for the *Illustrated London News* the life of a war artist in Zululand: 'Our Artist is an old campaigner, though still comparatively young in years, and his previous experience in Bulgaria and Bosnia, and in the Ashantee War, had made him tolerably indifferent to the danger of being under an enemy's fire' (18 October 1879). He described how combatants were amazed to see him sketching peacefully while a battle went on. He was not always so placid, and when he lost his sketchbook during the Battle of Ulundi, he burst into tears of frustration until a general lent him his own notebook.

Prince Louis Napoleon, son of the Empress Eugenie and the late Napoleon III of France,

had been at the Royal Military Academy, Woolwich, and volunteered for the Zulu War as he was anxious to put his military training into practice. The Government did not want him to go, but finally agreed only if he would act as a spectator not a combatant. Once in Zululand he became over-enthusiastic and the worst happened. Going ahead with a few men to make some topographical notes, the Prince's party was surprised by Zulus, and the survivors returned to camp without the Prince, who had last been seen unhorsed and surrounded. Prior was with the rescue party that found the body the next day. He described how the 'French correspondent leaning over with tears streaming down his face, took an English penny from his pocket and placed it over the Prince's eye.' Archibald Forbes, who was also present, wrote, 'To be slain by savages in an obscure corner of a remote continent was a miserable end, truly, for him who once was the Son of France.' Prior worked all night on his sketches and was gratified to discover that they were the first to arrive in London showing the event.

MELTON PRIOR

'The scene as the last of our men retreated from Majuba Hill, 27 February'
1880–1 IST BOER WAR
Wood engraving
Illustrated London News, 23 April 1881, p. 413

War had broken out in the Transvaal in 1880 as the Boers wished to regain their independence from British rule. Britain had scant respect for the Afrikaner army as a fighting force, an opinion they were soon forced to revise. Sir George Colley, who was leading the British advance, decided that the occupation of Majuba Hill would put his troops in a dominant position over the Boers. He commanded his men to scale the hill but neglected to tell them to dig in or to get their artillery into position.

John Cameron of the *Standard* was an eye-witness to the battle which followed. He said, 'The ascent was terribly difficult. The men, burdened with rifles and haversacks, had often to crawl on hands and knees. . . . The Naval Brigade endeavoured to hoist a Gatling gun, but found it an impossible task.' The Boers were able to surprise the party. The British panicked and fled down the hill. Cameron continues, 'Our advanced line was at once nearly all shot or driven in upon our main position. . . . At this moment I was knocked down by the rush and trampled on, and when I came to my senses the Boers were firing over me at the retreating troops, who were rushing down the hill. . . . Upon trying to rise I was taken prisoner.'

Prior arrived at Majuba 'just in time to see the remains of the troops coming down from the summit in a hasty retreat' (*Campaigns of a War Correspondent*). He got a careful description of events from Cameron, whom the Boers had released as a non-combatant, and from this composed his picture. 'Dear old Cameron was not much of an artist, but he gave me a lot of notes and rough sketches of the fight, which I was able to work up under his guidance and forward to England.'

Selling soldiers Kit Killed on Majuba Hill.
Mount Prospect Camp.
Boots, Jerseys, Coats, Shirts, Soap, Tobacco, Hold all, in variety of Articles.

MELTON PRIOR
'Selling kit of soldiers killed on Majuba Hill:
Mount Prospect Camp, May 1881'
1880–1 1ST BOER WAR
Original drawing
Pencil
National Army Museum

Sir George Colley was killed at Majuba with 93
of his men and 133 were wounded. Boer
casualties were only one dead and five wounded.
The wounded lay on the slopes of the hill
throughout the day after the fighting, and on the
following day an armistice was declared to clear
the battlefield. The Boers did not go on to attack
the base camp at Mount Prospect and it was here
that the wounded were received. The camp was
half-way between Laing's Nek and Schuins
Hooght, twelve miles out of Newcastle. Prior's
sketch, which does not appear to have been
published in the *Illustrated London News*, shows

the auction of boots, jerseys, coats, shirts, etc.,
belonging to the dead.

The British Government was furious at the
news of the defeat, and the public bewildered.
The Queen wrote, 'I do not like peace before we
have retrieved our honour.' Nevertheless
Gladstone negotiated a peace treaty, recognizing
the Transvaal's independence, although Britain
retained a nominal sovereignty. During peace
negotiations the war correspondents at Mount
Prospect Camp got tired of the inactivity, and
occupied themselves with sketching scenes of
camp life. Prior became depressed as some
packing cases labelled 'drawing materials',
actually containing whisky, had vanished. When
the Treaty of Pretoria was finally signed, Prior
was first with the news, and able to give the tip
to Cameron so that he too could get the news
back to the *Standard* ahead of his rival
correspondents.

MELTON PRIOR

'Lecture by Melton Prior on the battle of Tel-el-Kebir, 13 September 1882, illustrated by a slide of one of his sketches made on the spot'
1882 ARABI REBELLION
Photomechanical line engraving
Illustrated London News, 3 March 1883

A British expeditionary force was sent to Egypt in 1882 to put down the Arabi revolt which was threatening British interests in the country. The commander, Sir Garnet Wolseley, did not take the obvious route to Cairo, but attacked the Egyptian army's camp at Tel-el-Kebir in the desert, where he had a resounding victory. Prior arrived in Egypt in July. He was with John Cameron of the *Standard* at Tel-el-Kebir and they 'arrived just in time to see the troops storming the trenches.' Later they toured the battlefield together, and Prior offered a Highlander leaning in a trench a drink of whisky, but was horrified when the man lurched over dead.

On returning to England, Prior gave a lecture on the war at a Soirée attended by the Prince of Wales. 'It was listened to with unabated attention throughout; and the vivid battle scenes thrown by the lime-light on the screen presented a most interesting panorama of the naval and military operations of Lord Alcester and Lord Wolseley.' The slides illustrating the lecture were nearly all 'enlarged from the original sketches made by him under fire in Egypt. These were clearly thrown on the screen and each tableau was so bold and effective as to lend force to the illustration that Mr Prior was describing the stirring events as they happened before the spectators.' The Prince of Wales said, 'Everyone has known for years that Mr Melton Prior is a clever artist; but few probably were aware that he is so graphic a lecturer. I have just been told that this very interesting lecture has lasted an hour; but it seemed to me only ten minutes' (*Illustrated London News*, 3 March 1883).

About this time the first 'facsimile sketches' appear in the *Illustrated London News* as original drawings could now be transferred on to a block by photography.

Discipline a...

The Desert March

cene at the Wells of Aboo Halfa

ls no water for three scorching days.

the men had only a Pint in the morning & Pint at

vented a wild confusion setting in —

MELTON PRIOR
*'The desert march : scene at the wells of
Abou Halfa'*
1884–5 GORDON RELIEF EXPEDITION
Original drawing
Pencil
National Army Museum

While the British were occupied with the Arabi
revolt, trouble was brewing in the Sudan as a
result of the machinations of the religious leader
El Mahdi and his Dervish followers. Gordon was
isolated in Khartoum and a British relief force
under General Stewart set out to his rescue,
accompanied by a large number of
correspondents. For the newspapers this was the
great adventure story of the period, featuring a
gallant hero in distress, with the rescue party
having to face a fanatical enemy.

The Desert Column left the Nile at Korti to
cross two hundred miles of desert to Khartoum.
Frederic Villiers, who was with the press party,
has described the march to the wells of Abou
Halfa which were situated between Korti and
Gakdul: 'We have had a very trying and thirsty
march, such a terrible time I never have
experienced before. We have arrived here, and
there is water in plenty, but 'en route' we ran
very short, the men's allowance coming down to
two pints a day.' Prior described how some of
the water skins had leaked and said that 'we
arrived at the so-called wells of Abou Halfa
pretty well done up.' The men should have been
told to approach the well in batches but 'many of
the native drivers, with their natural indifference,
made a dash, and even waded into the pool, but
these were very soon hauled out, and in many
cases rather severely handled.'

It was difficult for correspondents to get their
despatches off, and Prior spent a good deal of
money bribing camel drivers to take his work
back to Korti. An engraving of Prior's sketch
appeared in the *Illustrated London News* on 21
February 1885.

MELTON PRIOR
'The battle of Abou Klea: repulse of the enemy from our square'
1884–5 GORDON RELIEF EXPEDITION
Original drawing
Black paint with yellow wash
National Army Museum

The Gordon Relief Column reached the wells at Abou Klea on 17 January 1885, where they were intercepted by the Dervishes. Henry Pearse, reporting the battle for the *Illustrated London News* on 7 February, said that the 19th Hussars when making a reconnaissance had found that the enemy was between them and the much-needed water. The column formed a square, and 'the brigade moved forward as steadily as if on parade'. They were harassed by the enemy during the night, and on the following morning the Dervishes attacked. The British formed a hollow square with the Guards in front, mounted infantry on the left flank, Sussex Regiment on the right, and the heavy cavalry and Naval Brigade in the rear. Camels, ammunition and hospital stretchers were in the centre. 'When we had time to look, we saw that line after line of the enemy had fallen under the Martini fire as they advanced. There could scarcely have been less than eight hundred or a thousand of dead and wounded Arabs.' The square did break at one point, but the Dervishes penetrating it were swiftly killed. The British were able to reach the wells where they bivouacked that night.

Prior and Cameron bribed a camel driver to take their despatches, but they did not arrive at their destination. When the *Illustrated London News* did not receive Prior's sketches as expected, their home-based artist, Caton Woodville, provided one of his highly imaginative illustrations of the battle. Luckily Prior had kept tracings of his drawings which he was able to send on later, but Cameron was killed in the next action, so his despatch was lost for ever.

Battle of Aboo Klea
Repulse of the enemy out of our Square

MELTON PRIOR
'Death of Mr Cameron'
1884–5 GORDON RELIEF EXPEDITION
Original drawing
Pencil
National Army Museum

Within sight of Metemmeh on 19 January General Stewart's Desert Column was again attacked by Dervishes. Stewart was wounded and there were casualties among the correspondents. Among those wounded were Bennet Burleigh of the *Telegraph*, Villiers of the *Graphic*, and Prior. Prior described how 'a bullet caught the instep of my boot, tearing it open, and then struck the heel of Villiers' boot as he sat cross-legged beside me'. A few seconds later Prior was grazed on the thumb by another bullet, Harry Pearce of the *Daily News* was hit, and John Cameron was killed. Prior said, 'He was sitting between camels eating sardines and biscuits when he received the fatal bullet and, with one gurgling sigh, fell back dead.' St Leger

Herbert of the *Morning Post* was killed in the same action. Wolseley, who had never thought much of Cameron, wrote in his journal: 'Our losses in killed and wounded have not been great. Poor St Leger Herbert shot through head. A braver soul never lived. Cameron, the *Standard* Correspondent of whom I cannot say the same, also killed' (*In Relief of Gordon*, edited by Adrian Preston).

Despite Wolseley's opinion, Cameron had held a place of affection among the other correspondents, who took charge of the burial party. A guard of honour was formed by Prior, Villiers, Burleigh, Pearse, Colonel Barrow of the Hussars and Lord Charles Beresford. Beresford read the Burial Service. With Stewart mortally wounded, Sir Charles Wilson took charge of the Desert Column, which did not reach Khartoum until 28 January, by which time Gordon had been dead for two days. Engravings of Cameron's death and the burial party appeared in the *Illustrated London News* on 28 February 1885.

MELTON PRIOR
'Mr Melton Prior, our special artist, sketching Dr Jameson in the prison in Pretoria'
1896 JAMESON RAID
'Facsimile sketch'
Photomechanical line engraving
Illustrated London News, 8 February 1896, p. 165

The discovery of gold in the Transvaal during the late 1880s brought an influx of new people, many of them British subjects, into the country. These 'uitlanders' were heavily taxed by President Kruger and had no vote. Misjudging their revolutionary fervour, Cecil Rhodes instigated a rebellion among them to overthrow Kruger's régime, timed to coincide with a raid across the border by his agent Dr Jameson. At the last moment Rhodes withdrew his support, sensing that the uitlanders would not carry out their part of the bargain, but Jameson unwisely carried on. The raiders were quickly intercepted by the Boers and defeated at Krugersdorp. Jameson escaped, but was captured at Doornkop and the Boer commander General Piet Cronje handed him over to the British for trial. Jameson was imprisoned, but the British public generally felt that it was a gallant attempt that failed.

Prior, who had been in South Africa reporting on the Gold Rush for the *Illustrated London News*, sketched the prisoners in the State Gaol at Pretoria. Jameson was in solitary confinement, and agreed to let Prior sketch him saying, 'That is all right, Prior: everyone knows you and your work.' He was 'in a tiny cell, reclining on a trestle bed, without comforts of any kind, with the exception of cigarettes and matches. In the corner was an old wine box on which was a tin washing bowl, and a tin jug was on the ground. There was also a bottle with a candle stuck in it'. The other prisoners looked more comfortable 'and had every luxury possible, including fruit of all descriptions, champagne, brandy, whisky, soda-water, and even ice. . . . They pass the time by playing poker with matches, which represent two shillings each, and in the evening they play at marbles.' They were all pleased to see Prior who knew most of them 'for they were all members of the Rand Club. I must own that, barring the bad sleeping quarters and the fact that they were in prison, they were jolly comfortable' (*Campaigns of a War Correspondent*).

Death of Mr Cameron, Correspondent of the "Standard" at the Battle of Abu Klea.

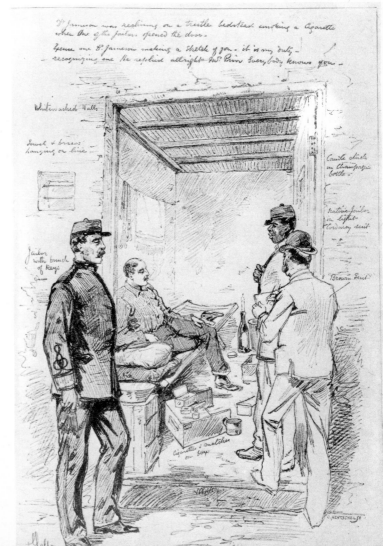

Dr Jameson was reclining on a trestle bedstead smoking a cigarette when one of the jailors opened the door.

"I see one Dr Jameson making a sketch of you - it is my duty" - recognising one He replied allright Mr Prior Everybody knows you -

Whitewashed Walls

Towel & braces hanging on line

Jailor with bunch of keys

Candle stick in Champagne bottle

native jailor in light corduroy suit

Brown Tent

Cigarettes & matches on soap

MELTON PRIOR

'A false alarm in Buluwayo : townspeople rushing into a laager'

1896 2ND MATABELE WAR

'Facsimile sketch'

Photomechanical line engraving

Illustrated London News, 6 June 1896, p. 728

The Matabele, whose land had been annexed by
Cecil Rhodes in 1890, made two ineffectual
attempts at rebellion. In 1893 the uprising had
been firmly suppressed but in 1896 the tribe rose
again, attacking isolated farms and massacring
the inhabitants. The garrison at Buluwayo was
surrounded by a force twenty times as large, and
a British expedition set out to relieve the town.
Among those accompanying the force were Cecil
Rhodes and Lt. Colonel Baden-Powell, who later
described the campaign as 'the happiest days of
my life'.

At Buluwayo a laager was constructed in the
market square, in the centre of which was the
Town Hall where the women and children were
accommodated. There was a line of wagons
outside the building, then a passage and beyond
this a double row of wagons, the outside ones
being sandbagged. Barbed wire surrounded the
construction. Prior was in Buluwayo during the
siege and said that there were several false alarms
of Matabele attacks, when men, women and
children rushed for cover while volunteers
manned the perimeter.

The artist Charlie Fripp, who was covering
the campaign for the *Graphic*, was with the relief
column and described how 'refugees from
Buluwayo flocked on the road. These folk spoke
ill of the administration of Matabeleland; the
natives, they said, were in a state of constant
discontent, and had seized the opportunity of the
departure of forces under Dr Jameson to avenge
themselves' (*Graphic*, 15 August 1896).
However, the Matabele were no match for the
British guns, and in spite of support from a
neighbouring tribe, the Mashona, were
compelled to give in.

A false alarm in Buluwayo. Townspeople rushing into Laager.

MELTON PRIOR
'Disaster of the Dorset Regiment'
1897 TIRAH VALLEY EXPEDITION
Original drawing
Pencil
National Army Museum

In the words of their commander, Sir William Lockhart, the purpose of the British expedition to the Tirah, on the North-West Frontier of India, was to 'march through the country of the Afridis and Oraksais and to announce from the heart of the country the final terms which will be imposed. The advance is made to mark the power of the British Government to advance if and when they choose.' Prior and René Bull of *Black and White* messed together during the expedition, and Prior recalled in his memoirs how they had dug a hole for their tent in the Maidan Valley and 'succeeded in making ourselves absolutely safe from bullets. Here we made our sketches, here we slept, while we heard the whiz and the ping of the little bits of lead flying over heads.'

The incident in the sketch occurred on 16 November when General Kempster's brigade was crossing the Tseri-Kandoa Pass. The 15th Sikhs were attacked by Afridis on the northern side of the ridge and the 36th Sikhs were sent to their aid, followed by two companies of the Dorset Regiment. Night was falling and more than half the Dorsetshire force was cut off in a nullah by the enemy 'who poured fierce fire upon them from the adjoining heights, and then descended to close quarters' (*Illustrated London News*, 18 December 1897). The Dorsetshires fought bravely, losing two officers and thirteen men before they were able to join up with the 36th Sikhs.

Destroying homes and crops indiscriminately on their journey as reprisal measures, the British at length negotiated with the tribesmen and started on the return march. The total British casualties on the expedition were 1,300 and in fact little had been accomplished as only a few Afridi tribes paid the fines imposed in the settlement. A very inferior version of Prior's sketch, redrawn by H. C. Seppings Wright, was published in the *Illustrated London News* on 18 December 1897.

Night scene Enemy on top of Mullah

Enemy falling back

The Torch Expedition

Melton Prior

The Disaster to the Dorset Regiments
Hand to hand fighting with the Enemy
in a Mullah —

MELTON PRIOR

'Mutiny of the Mussulman Gendarmes in Canea : Colonel Bor endeavouring to control the mutineers, and their Colonel, Suleiman Bey, shot dead'
1897 TURKO–GREEK WAR (CRETE)
Facsimile
Photomechanical line engraving
Illustrated London News, 20 March 1897, p. 394

Crete had not been able to obtain her freedom from the Turks when the new Greek state was proclaimed in 1832. At length after a relatively minor incident in 1898 involving loss of life among British soldiers stationed on the island, the Great Powers stepped in and forced the Turks to leave Crete, giving it autonomous status under a High Commissioner, Prince George of Greece.

Prior was present when the Turkish gendarmerie mutinied against their hated Colonel, Suleiman Bey. The English admiral had sent Colonel Bor of the Marines on shore to maintain order, and Italian bluejackets also landed and surrounded the barracks, ordering the gendarmes to put down their arms. The gendarmes promptly shot Suleiman, much to the consternation of several correspondents, including Prior, who were upstairs and thought that the mutineers would be after them next. Colonel Bor would have been in difficulties had it not been for the Italians who were able to restore order. In Prior's sketch Colonel Bor is on the right of the door, with Captain Churchill, another British officer, beside him.

MELTON PRIOR

'The Battle of Lombard's Kop. Reverend Macpherson and Mr Smith (Morning Leader) *visiting the wounded after the surrender of the Gloucesters and Irish Fusiliers'*
1899–1902 BOER WAR
Facsimile
Photomechanical line engraving
Illustrated London News, 9 December 1899, p. 823, bottom

Prior was in Natal during the early stages of the Boer War and was in action at Elandslaagte in October 1899. He was nervous that his white helmet would draw enemy fire, but 'realised that if I took it off my bald head would act like a heliograph to them'. He solved the problem by going into battle with a cloak over his head.

After Elandslaagte, General Yule's army fell back to Ladysmith, arriving there on 26 October. The Boers closed in, and in a last desperate attempt to break the circle, the British commander at Ladysmith, Sir George White, sent out a column to engage the Boers at Nicholson's Nek, seven miles north of the town. The battle was a disaster for the British. The Irish Fusiliers, Gloucesters and No. 10 Mountain Battery were surrounded on Kainguba Heights and subjected to intense Boer rifle fire, finally being forced to surrender. Deneys Reitz, fighting with the Pretoria Commando, described the dead and wounded soldiers saying that 'the cries and groans of agony, and the dreadful sights, haunted me for many a day, for though I had seen death by violence of late, there had been nothing to approach the horrors accumulated here.' On his way back to the town Prior met up with Bennet Burleigh, who cried, 'Prior, my boy, it is all over – we are beaten, and it means investment. We shall all be locked up in Ladysmith!' On the morning after the battle the Boers sent an envoy, under the flag of truce, saying that the dead and wounded could be dealt with, and the Reverend Macpherson went out to arrange this, accompanied by Smith of the *Morning Leader*. Prior followed to make sketches. Prior's letter to the *Illustrated London News* says, 'We are practically invested in Ladysmith. I am sending this down to Maritzburg with two other correspondents' letters by special Kaffir messenger, as I did my last, and I hope they will all get through.'

Prior was confined in Ladysmith with the rest of the garrison until March. He did not return to England until July 1900, when it was reported, 'It is a curious irony of fate that Mr Prior should have escaped Shot and Shell at Ladysmith to be wounded in the eye by a cricket ball during his voyage home.'

Mutiny of the Mussulman Gendarmes in Canea, Crete.
Suleiman Bey (their Colonel) shot dead.
Colonel Bor trying to stop the mutineers.

The Battle of Lombard's Kop.
The Revd Macpherson and Mr Smith of the Morning Leader visiting the wounded after the surrender of the Gloucesters & Irish Fusiliers.

ANON

1899–1902 BOER WAR
National Army Museum

A caricature of 'A War Artist at the Front'
during the Boer War which appeared in *The
Regiment*, 27 January 1900. The artist is having
the same trouble as Melton Prior with his helmet
and has hopefully placed it on a rock to draw the
fire.

JOHANN NEPOMUK SCHÖNBERG
(1844–?)
'Scene before the druggist's shop at Pirot'
1885 SERVO-BULGARIAN WAR
Facsimile
Photomechanical line engraving
Illustrated London News, 26 December 1885,
p. 662 top

'John' Schönberg, born in Austria in 1844, was
son of the engraver and lithographer Adolf
Schönberg. He studied at the Academy of
Vienna and at Munich and worked for *Le Monde
Illustré* and other French illustrated papers. He
first represented the *Illustrated London News* in
1866, reporting from the Austrian side on the
war with Prussia, while his colleague on the
journal, Robert Landells, was with the Prussians.

After the war Schönberg occasionally sent
sketches of Viennese life to the *Illustrated London

News*, and his next campaign as the journal's
representative was the Servo-Turkish War of
1875–6, followed by the Russo-Turkish War of
1877–8. After some service in Egypt he went to
join the Serbian forces in their struggle with
Bulgaria in 1885. He arrived at the beginning of
November, shortly before the battles of Slivnica
and Pirot. The Bulgarians defeated the Serbs at
Slivnica on 17 November, pushing them back to
Pirot. Here the Bulgarians attacked again on 27
November and an armistice was called on 28
November after the Serbs had retreated in
disorder with heavy casualties. Schönberg's
sketch shows the wounded seeking help at an
apothecary's shop during the fighting.

JOHANN NEPOMUK SCHÖNBERG
'Boer sharpshooters on Proctor's Kopje, near Ladysmith'
1899–1902 BOER WAR
Facsimile
Photomechanical line engraving
Sphere 5 May 1900, p. 469

A new British illustrated paper, the *Sphere*, obtained Schönberg's services as artist-correspondent at the Boer War. He was persuaded by the journal to pose as the representative of a German paper and was thus given preferential treatment at the Boer headquarters. Joubert himself placed his carriage at Schönberg's disposal and for a while the *Sphere* received unique despatches which they captioned 'from our correspondent on the Boer side', in discreet anonymity. This happy state of affairs might have continued but for a tactless telegram sent by the *Sphere* to Schönberg asking him not to leave the Boer camp where he was finding life rather a strain. The telegram ended with the words 'London requests you to remain'. The Boers promptly smelt a rat and expelled Schönberg from their headquarters.

His sketch of Boer sharpshooters near Ladysmith at Proctor's Kopje shows the men behind boulders shooting at the British infantry. In the foreground there are shell holes caused by artillery fire. A few months later Schönberg was wounded at Pretoria and went home.

JOHANN NEPOMUK SCHÖNBERG

'Captain Soady and his detachment of Sikhs climbing the walls of Peking'

1900 BOXER REBELLION
Facsimile
Photomechanical half-tone engraving
Illustrated London News, 24 November 1900, p. 771

On 14 July 1900 the *Illustrated London News* reported that they had commissioned Schönberg to represent them in China, where there was trouble reported from the Boxers. By August the journal was publishing Schönberg's sketches from the Suez area. The length of the voyage and the problems of sending despatches home meant that the *Illustrated London News* received nothing of use from their 'special' until November, by which time all the excitement had died down. When the allies reached Peking at the end of August, the journal had to rely on imaginative reconstructions of events by Caton Woodville and other staff artists. By October some

photographs from other correspondents were beginning to come through, but all Schönberg's work was published in late November and he may well have travelled back with his sketches rather than try to send them by post. The artist had been able to visit all the places concerned, but naturally relied on verbal accounts for the actual fighting.

In this picture an officer of the Engineers, Captain Soady, climbs the Peking wall barefoot, unwinding his turban to use as a flag. The Sikhs were then able to open the Inner Gate and allow the Germans, Russians and Japanese to come in. 'That is an old story now; but memories of all sorts, some of them very heroic ones, will long cling to the scenes Mr Schönberg has portrayed', records the *Illustrated London News* on 24 November 1900. Another drawing by Schönberg in the same issue shows Major Scott leading a different party by way of the watergate towards the Legations.

WALTER PAGET
*'The War in the Soudan: the march to Tamai
– inflating the balloon'*
1884–5 GORDON RELIEF EXPEDITION
Photomechanical line engraving, redrawn
Illustrated London News, 2 May 1885, p. 455

Walter Paget and his brother Sidney were well-
known illustrators who worked for books and the
picture papers. Walter Paget's only campaign as
a war correspondent appears to have been the
Gordon Relief Expedition, where he provided
some interesting sketches of camp life which the
Illustrated London News reproduced in facsimile.
He was with General Sir Gerald Graham's army
at the British base of Suakin on the Red Sea, and
accompanied them to Tamai in 1884. His picture
shows the observation balloon being inflated.
Balloons had been used for reconnaissance since
the time of the American Civil War and,
although cumbersome, did sometimes save the
lives of scouts. Major Temple and Lieutenant
Mackenzie of the Royal Engineers were in
charge of this balloon and the gas was 'carried
in tubes compressed into 75 volumes. . . . The
balloon is made of gold-beaters' skin, is 23 ft in
diameter, contains 7,000 ft cubic of gas, and its
total weight is 90 lbs. It is attached by a rope
200 ft long to a wagon or any other convenient
holdfast; one of the officers goes up in the car,
and thence commands a very extensive view.
Messages are sent up and down, written on small
pieces of paper attached to the rope by a sliding
loop. The gas is brought from England, having
been manufactured at Chatham and the balloon
can remain aloft during nine hours.'

Among the books that Walter Paget illustrated
were *Treasure Island* (1899), *Pilgrim's Progress*
(1906) and *Arabian Nights* (1907). He and his
brother became staff artists for the *Sphere* when
it was founded in 1900.

FRANK ALGERNON STEWART
(1877–?)
'How Lord Roberts's son fell: saving the guns at Colenso, 15 December 1899'
1899–1902 BOER WAR
Facsimile
Photomechanical line engraving
Illustrated London News, 20 January 1900, p. 75

Frank Stewart covered General Buller's march to relieve Ladysmith during the Boer War in the absence of the *Illustrated London News's* chief correspondent, Melton Prior, who was among those besieged. The column attacked the Boers at Colenso on 15 December and the 14th and 66th Batteries, Royal Artillery, were forced to abandon their guns. Buller called for volunteers to recapture them. Men quickly came forward and included Corporal Nurse, six drivers, all of the 66th Battery, and two officers. One of the officers was Lieutenant the Hon. Fred S. Roberts of the 60th Rifles, ADC to General Clery and the only son of Field-Marshal Roberts. The party managed to recover two of the guns but Roberts was hit. He was brought back and taken to the hospital at Chievely, but he was mortally wounded and died on 16 December. He was awarded a posthumous VC.

Stewart's sketch shows Corporal Nurse in the centre leading a horse, with Lieutenant Roberts on the right. A corporal of the 66th Battery, probably Nurse, has described what happened: 'I got the horses over to the limber, and Lord Roberts's son held my horse while I helped to hook in. As soon as I got them mounted I started off at a gallop for the guns, half a mile away. The enemy were following us with a perfect storm of shot and shell, one of which burst overhead just before we mounted and took the off-centre's eye clean out. Lord Roberts's son was shot as we were going up.' The party was able to secure two of the guns but 'the bullets were pattering around us like hail. . . . I got the two guns back safely, despite the heavy fire we experienced going and coming' (quoted in Kenneth Griffith, *Thank God We Kept the Flag Flying*). There were five VCs awarded.

Stewart's only service as a war correspondent was at the Boer War. He later became a specialist in painting and illustrating hunting scenes, pursuing 'the image of war without its guilt and only five and twenty per cent of its danger' (Introduction to his book, *Cross Country With Hounds*).

FREDERIC VILLIERS (1852–1922)
'Scene in a wood, near Tesica, Servia'
1875–6 SERVO–TURKISH WAR
Wood engraving, redrawn by G. Durand
Graphic, 16 September 1876, p. 265

Frederic Villiers was Melton Prior's counterpart on the *Graphic* and his career covered much the same span. He was only twenty-four and fresh from art school when he offered his services as a war artist to the manager of the *Graphic*, William Thomas. He was sent to Serbia 'with a bag of sovereigns in my pocket and a letter from my editor to Mr Archibald Forbes' (Frederic Villiers, *Pictures of Many Wars*). Forbes was already famous as a correspondent and the introduction was the beginning of a life-long friendship.

Villiers was soon in action and in the evenings helped Forbes with the wounded, 'by passing the instruments from one room to another, holding a candle, or pressing the hand of some poor creature under operation' (*Villiers: His Five Decades of Adventure*). Bosnia and Herzegovina were in revolt against Turkey and in 1875 were joined by Montenegro, Serbia and Bulgaria. The Turkish army was too strong for the Slavs, and each day Villiers could see the glow in the sky 'for the Turks were always victorious, and destroyed everything that came in their way as they advanced'.

His illustration is unusually horrific for an age which shrank from realism in the depiction of war. Forbes described in the *Daily News* how the Turks were burning every village in the Morava Valley and that 'Mr Villiers, of the *Graphic*, was shown near Tesica three Servians who had been found wounded. They were tied to trees with ropes, and roasted to death with fires lighted under them.' The Turks did not respect the Red Cross, and terrible atrocities were inflicted by the Circassians and Bashi Bazouks. When the *Graphic* published the picture the commentary said: 'The subject is a very repulsive one, but we feel it to be our duty at the present time not to shrink from representing an incident of this kind.'

An armistice was signed in the early winter of 1876, and Villiers received instructions to leave for India, but the plan was quickly changed when Russia declared war on Turkey and Villiers was asked to cover the Turkish side. He was rather apprehensive about his reception in Constantinople after the reports he had sent in about Turkish atrocities but 'luckily, in those days names of artists were seldom published below their sketches, so I was known but little. . . .'

FREDERIC VILLIERS
'Archibald Forbes, the war correspondent'
? 1877–8 RUSSO–TURKISH WAR
Original drawing
Pencil
National Portrait Gallery

There is a war correspondent in Rudyard Kipling's *The Light that Failed* who always opens his conversation with the gambit, there would be 'trouble in the Balkans in the spring'. The description could apply equally to Villiers or Forbes, both of whom became very involved in the progress of Slavonic freedom. This sketch of Forbes was probably completed in 1876 or 1877 when the two men were in the Balkans together as correspondents. They were both spectators at the Battle of Plevna in July 1877 and Villiers watched Forbes writing his report while the battle raged round him. Forbes was equally impressed by Villiers's bravery and his ability to produce sketches 'in desperate haste under fire', which could not be tidied up in any

way afterwards as Forbes would take them immediately with his own work for despatch from Bucharest (*Graphic*, 6 December 1890).

Forbes had first become a war correspondent during the Franco–Prussian War when he was sent to Metz by the *Morning Advertiser*. He changed over to the *Daily News* shortly afterwards and there made his name. Forbes excelled in being first with the news, and at Plevna arranged for a series of horses to be ready at different points so that he could ride non-stop over 140 miles to deliver his report. This became a habit, and he made another epic ride from Ulundi in 1800 carrying news of the victory over the Zulu chief, Cetshwayo. He was a bad-tempered man, but always remained on good terms with Villiers although he complained about Villiers's habit of going to bed with his spurs on. Villiers wrote in his memoirs, 'After a campaign I would very often join my friend and confrère, Archibald Forbes, in the Highlands of Scotland for fishing and shooting.'

FREDERIC VILLIERS

'Tiffin with an Afghan chief at Gandamak'
1878–80 2ND AFGHAN WAR
Wood engraving
Graphic, 21 June 1879, p. 597 bottom

Villiers had a difficult journey from Jellalabad to
join Sir Sam Browne's division advancing
towards Kabul through the Khyber Pass. The
heat was intense, his pony's feet got blistered and
'the rocks glowed like huge live coals in the fierce
glint of the dying sun. The air was so thick and
nauseating with the stench of dead camels, that
one could hardly breathe' (*Pictures of Many
Wars*). Afghanistan had first been occupied by
the British in 1842 and any signs of
independence by the Amir were always instantly
crushed as Russian infiltration was feared. Yakub
Khan agreed to negotiate peace terms in May
1879.

Soon after this Major Cavagnari, leader of the
peace mission, invited Villiers to go with a party
to breakfast with the Khan of Gandamak. The
Khan did not bear any grudges and felt that the
British had defeated the Afghans in a fair fight
and 'why not be the best of friends?' Villiers
gave an account of the breakfast to the *Graphic*.
'After at least an hour's chat a servant produced
a few cucumbers in a soiled handkerchief, which
did not seem to meet with great success, as they
were placed upon a charpoy untouched, and
were afterwards sat down upon by one of the
guests.' Twenty minutes passed, marked only by
the arrival of two bunches of flowers. Finally a
waterproof cloth was laid on the table and
breakfast proper commenced. 'Two "chupattis"
or large flat cakes of unleavened bread were
placed before each of us, one to eat and the other
to serve as a plate.' Hard-boiled eggs were
distributed, 'and the cooks now arrived with
pieces of kid, fowl, and mutton frizzling on long
spits. . . . Forced meats and pilaus' followed, and
'sweet tea in florid, curious china cups, and
toasted cheese finished the repast.' It was a pity
after such lavish hospitality that Cavagnari was
murdered by his hosts four months later, and
war started again.

FREDERIC VILLIERS
'*After the burning of Alexandria; our artist and the* Standard *correspondent visiting the Grand Square during the conflagration*'
1882 ARABI REBELLION
Wood engraving
Graphic, 5 August 1882, p. 121 bottom

After the building of the Suez Canal in 1869, Britain and France began to increase their influence in Egypt as the power of Turkey declined. In 1882 Colonel Ahmed Arabi organized a revolt with the purpose of deposing the inept Khedive, and throwing foreigners out of the country. In June there were riots at Alexandria in which a number of Europeans were killed, which provided an excuse for the British to send in gunboats and an ultimatum to Arabi. Villiers arrived at Alexandria in June and was given quarters on the British gunboat *Condor*. Acting on a tip-off from a friend he was able to sketch the new cannon that Arabi was installing in the main fort of Alexandria, contrary to the conditions of the ultimatum.

He was a witness to the subsequent bombardment of the city and quite enjoyed the occasion. 'The episode of the *Condor* was one of the pleasantest I have ever taken part in. There was no blood or hurt about it – at least with us'

(*Pictures of Many Wars*). He was able to watch the gunners who 'became as black as negroes with the powder, and were compelled to continually dip their heads in the sponge buckets to keep the grit from their eyes'. After it was over he went on shore with John Cameron of the *Standard*, who had been reporting the event from the *Chiltern*, in between bouts of fearful sea sickness. They went to the Grand Square where all the finest European stores had been, which Villiers described as 'one vast mass of glowing fire. The crashing noise of the falling walls, and the crackling sound of the flames as they leapt and encircled fresh houses, added to the weirdness of the scene. . . . The rumble of the burning buildings as they flared and toppled to the ground; the hissing of steam as the melting leaden piping let loose jets of water into the burning debris, and the howls and screams of frightened animals made the night hideous' (*Villiers : His Five Decades of Adventure*). It was particularly eery to hear the sap in the trees hissing, and Cameron was alarmed to see what he thought were mutilated bodies in the centre of the Square. Luckily these turned out to be dressmakers' dummies.

FREDERIC VILLIERS

'Wreck of the press boat "Georgie" : Mr F. Villiers and Mr Charles Williams rescued from drowning by the pinnace of the "Inflexible"'

1884–5 GORDON RELIEF EXPEDITION
Wood engraving
Graphic, 24 January 1885, p. 80 bottom

After Arabi had been defeated, the British reconstituted the Egyptian army on British lines under British officers. At the same time Britain inherited from Egypt the problems of the Sudan, which were to remain a source of trouble until the end of the century. Gordon had allowed himself to be besieged in Khartoum by the followers of the Mahdi, and every war correspondent of note joined the relief expedition. The party moved up the Nile by boat and Villiers and Williams were among the many who had narrow escapes from drowning in the murky waters of the river.

On 20 December 1884 Villiers described in the *Graphic* the departure from Dongola. 'There was a sort of Chinese piratical junk-like appearance about the scene as the boats quickly filled, and floated out into the middle of the Nile.' Charles Williams of *Central News* had brought a whaler from England and Villiers joined him for the journey. It was not easy, as Williams later said, because of 'the shifting sandbanks, the movements of which at this season are always uncertain, and are this year, we learn, unusually eccentric.' Caught in cross-currents, the boat capsized and Villiers was lucky to get away with his life as he was swept underneath the vessel, and had at the time been wearing top-boots and an overcoat, 'and was so heavily weighted that I rose only sufficiently to take my last look round' (*Pictures of Many Wars*).

All of Villiers's precious gear was lost: 'my bed furniture, tea, sugar, canned beef, tobacco, a bottle of pickles, a pepper mill, an extra pair of boots, a dispatch case, and a bag of sixty sovereigns. . . . It was a catastrophe of which only campaigners can appreciate the bitterness. I knew that my personal comfort was also wrecked for many months to come, for there were no shops or stores handy in the wilds of the Soudan.' Villiers and Williams were picked up by Lieutenant Montgomerie of the *Inflexible*, although there was some delay as the rescue party's boat got caught on a sandbank, and they had to shoot at the crocodiles to keep them away from the unfortunate journalists. They spent a damp night on the banks of the Nile before walking thirty miles the next day to Korti, where they were given new clothes and equipment.

ANON
'Mr Villiers becomes an object of compassion'
1884–5 GORDON RELIEF EXPEDITION
Original watercolour
National Army Museum

One of a series of seven watercolours by an
amateur artist in the possession of the National
Army Museum, this painting shows Frederic
Villiers after falling in the Nile again on the
journey back to Dongola. He was travelling on
the *Nassif-il-Kir* which hit a submerged rock
near Debbeh and sank. He was carried by the
river on to a sandbank, where an irrigation wheel
was 'creaking and moaning', and when he
regained consciousness he was surrounded by
Sudanese women, which caused him some
embarrassment as his 'only garment was a flannel
cricket shirt' (*Pictures of Many Wars*).

FREDERIC VILLIERS
'*Taking the key of Port Arthur – the
Japanese attack on Fort Esioyama*'
1894–5 SINO-JAPANESE WAR
Photomechanical half-tone engraving, redrawn by
Ernest Prater
Black and White 19 January 1895, p. 72

For the ten years following the Gordon Relief
Expedition, Villiers divided his time between
lecture tours and free-lance work. He was in the
Balkans again in 1885 for the *Graphic* during the
Servo-Bulgarian War, and also covered the 3rd
Burma War for the journal.

In 1894 China and Japan were in conflict over
the control of Korea and fighting broke out in
July. Villiers, laden with kit, set out in August
representing *Black and White*, but it took some
time before he arrived in the battle zone. He

joined the Japanese of whom he said, 'I have had experience of most European armies and I think the Japs have no reason to fear comparison with the best of them.' He particularly asked it to be stated that he was the only combat artist with the Japanese army, saying that there was a Frenchman (presumably George Bigot of the *Graphic*) pretending to be sending sketches from the Japanese front line. According to Villiers, this man was sending his drawings from Chemulpo, a treaty port 'not within the sphere of Chinese bullets.' He indignantly continued, 'Those who honestly try to give true illustrations of the war, risk their lives, drink prison water and eat little but rice for days together, while these cowardly charlatans concoct sketches from photographs and telegrams in the easeful security of a neutral port' (*Black and White*, 1 December 1894).

Port Arthur was taken after three days fighting. The fort was one of two guarding the entrance to the Gulf of Pechili, which led to Taku and the traditional route up the Peiho to Peking. General Yamagi's division, accompanied by Villiers, advanced towards Fort Esioyama on the morning of 21 November 1894. The attack was at 7.00 a.m. 'There was a terrible fire for a short time, but in fifteen minutes from the start the Japs rushed the works and planted their flags in the enemy's largest redoubt, finding that only twenty-five Chinamen had remained to dispute its possession.' When the Japanese entered Port Arthur at 3.30 p.m. they saw the severed heads of some of their comrades and gave way to indiscriminate slaughter of the Chinese.

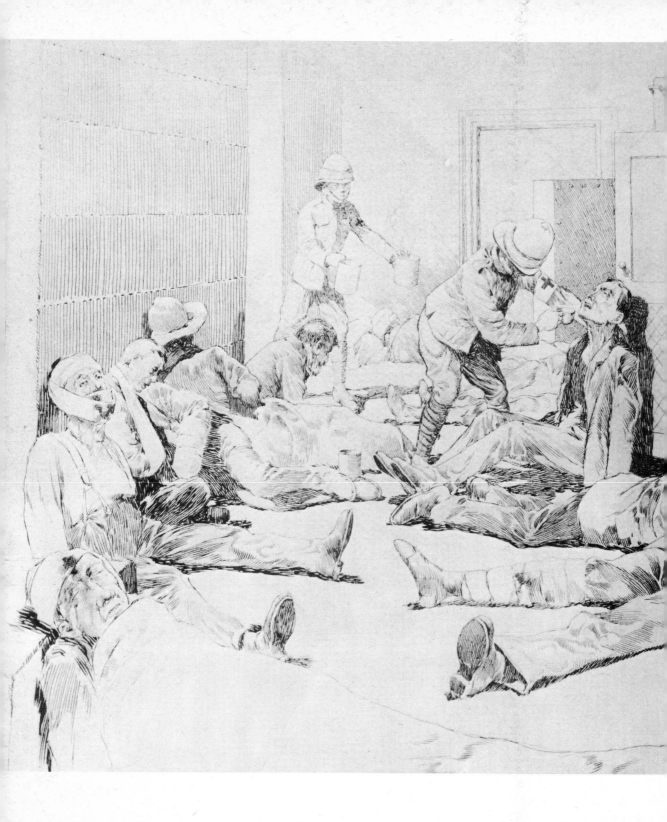

FREDERIC VILLIERS

'With the Kimberley Relief Column after the battle of Speyfontein: succouring the Boer wounded in the Crown and Royal Hotel, Modder River'

1899–1902 BOER WAR

Photomechanical line engraving, redrawn

Illustrated London News, 13 January 1900, p. 40

Villiers returned to the Balkans in 1897 for the Greek campaign against Turkey and the following year he joined Kitchener's advance on Omdurman. A lecture tour in Australia followed, but he left hurriedly for South Africa on hearing about the outbreak of the Boer War in 1899. Villiers probably acted as a free-lance in South Africa and this time sent his work to the *Illustrated London News*. He joined Lord Methuen's force for the relief of Kimberley saying, 'From the first it struck me that, from the journalistic point of view, the relief of Kimberley and the rescue of Cecil Rhodes would probably be the most interesting thing to see.'

This picture, which has been redrawn by a staff artist, shows the aftermath of the Battle of Magersfontein on 28 November 1899. The action was a bad defeat for the British who were forced to retreat to Modder River Station, where Villiers was able to sketch some Boer casualties. Among the wounded were men of the Scandinavian corps under Baron Fadersewold. Only seven out of eighty of these men had escaped injury. Kimberley was relieved in February 1900 after the battle of Paardeberg and Villiers was able to sketch the defeated Boer leader, Cronje, and his wife 'a meek little lady looking rather bedraggled in a black silk dress covered with dust.' He also ungallantly sketched for the *Illustrated London News* a young British officer finding Mrs Cronje's corsets abandoned on the battlefield.

Villiers remained in South Africa until after Pretoria was taken. His days as a war artist were not yet over and he played an active part in the Russo-Japanese War of 1904–5, and in 1914 joined the French army, serving throughout the First World War.

GEORGE BIGOT

'After the battle at Ping Yang : a corner of the field of battle'
1894–5 SINO–JAPANESE WAR
Facsimile
Photomechanical line engraving
Graphic, 1 December 1894, p. 621

Little is known about George Bigot, who was the *Graphic*'s representative on the Japanese side during the Sino–Japanese War of 1894–5. Bigot was a Frenchman, probably resident in China, and he produced some moving and elegant sketches of the battlefields. Frederic Villiers claimed that Bigot never saw action, but it is difficult to see how he could have produced drawings of such quality from photographs. His pictures in fact appear much more true to life than Villiers's own work which is never reproduced in facsimile, but always redrawn by a staff artist.

Ping Yang in Korea was the scene of one of the opening battles of the war, in August 1894. The town was a Chinese stronghold on the Tatung River, on the road from the Korean capital to the Manchurian frontier. The Japanese moved forward to attack the fort after their victory at Asan, and by 2.00 p.m. on 5 August 1894 had forced the defenders to surrender. Bigot's sketch shows the Japanese troops making their Chinese prisoners carry off the dead and wounded. Bigot continued with the Japanese army during their march on Seoul and spoke admiringly of 'Japanese pluck and energy versus Chinese weakness and cowardice'.

In the spring of 1895 the *Graphic* published several coloured reproductions of Bigot's work showing typical Korean characters. The journal had been using colour for special Summer and Christmas issues since the 1880s.

HENRY CHARLES SEPPINGS WRIGHT (d.1937)

'The advance towards Dongola – cholera in the camp; in quarantine'

1896–8 RECONQUEST OF THE SUDAN
Photomechanical half-tone engraving, redrawn
Illustrated London News, 22 August 1896, p. 244
bottom

H. C. Seppings Wright had served in the Navy and later turned to art for a living. Between 1883 and 1888 he exhibited landscapes at the Suffolk Street Gallery and the New Gallery, and at one time or another worked as an illustrator for most of the picture papers. He was a 'special' for the *Illustrated London News* at the Ashanti Expedition and on his return was sent to Egypt to join Kitchener's advance on Dongola in the spring of 1896. On arriving at Aswan he purchased three camels at £15 each, 'one to ride and two to place my baggage on'. He settled with other correspondents in a Dervish house but cholera broke out, and 'the Sirdar at once gave orders to move the camp to Kosheh, eight miles south; and, on the following morning I rode over with dear old "Peary", my "bitter foe" of the

Graphic, to select our new quarters,' recorded Seppings Wright in his memoirs. The correspondents gave a dinner party in their new accommodation, feasting on goose and hare shot by Beaman of the *Standard*. They were worried the next day when the groom working for Pearse of the *Graphic* died of cholera, and camp was moved again, this time into the desert where this sketch was made. The artist has drawn himself and a colleague on the left of the picture.

There were many deaths from cholera during the days which followed, the victims including Garrett of the *New York Herald*, and those not seriously ill generally had dysentery. Soon afterwards there was a sand storm and Seppings Wright wrote, 'our papers and sketches were blown over the desert, and our horses got loose and galloped about. Our nice-looking little camp was a scene of utter desolation'.

The following year Seppings Wright represented the *Illustrated London News* in Greece, and his later campaigns included the Spanish–American War and the Russo–Japanese War. He wrote several books about his experiences, and was at the Russian and French fronts during the First World War.

RENÉ BULL (d.1942)
'Arrest of an Armenian in Constantinople'
1895–6 ARMENIAN MASSACRES
Facsimile
Photomechanical half-tone engraving
Black and White, 5 December 1896, p. 713

When *Black and White* was first published in London, in 1890, the intention was to use photographs when possible rather than sketches. The journal was printed on good quality paper which showed illustrations of all kinds to the best advantage. René Bull was one of *Black and White*'s first war correspondents and he combined the roles of writer, artist and photographer. In January 1897 the *Ludgate Magazine* described him as having been a pupil of Caran D'Ache, 'and for some years everyone has known him as the author of numerous stories told in sketches without the aid of words. It remained for *Black and White* to discover that he was capable of work vastly more serious. As its Special Artist in Constantinople he has displayed artistic powers that have until now been latent, and a pluck and courage that make him an ideal special correspondent'.

Bull's first assignment was to report on the Armenian massacres and when he arrived at the Pera Hotel, Constantinople he was welcomed to the war correspondents' clan by Melton Prior. *Black and White* reported, 'Despite extreme difficulties, for a camera is strictly prohibited, Mr Bull by the exercise of great ingenuity has taken some excellent photographs, nor has his pencil been idle.' The Armenian in his drawings was arrested opposite his hotel. Bull writes, 'He gave the police such a twisting that it took them all their time to hold him; he fought like a lion, keeping up the while the most piercing shrieks imaginable. I must add, however, that they almost shook the life out of him. I wonder if he will ever be heard of again.' By the end of the year the immediate trouble in Armenia was dying down, and Bull went to India to report on the Bombay plague.

RENÉ BULL
'The Northamptons bringing in their dead'
1897–8 TIRAH VALLEY EXPEDITION
Facsimile
Photomechanical half-tone engraving
Black and White, 18 December 1897, p. 764

When war broke out between Greece and Turkey in 1897, Bull covered the campaign for *Black and White* and, with Bennet Burleigh of the *Daily Telegraph*, was among the last to leave Larissa. Afterwards, writing of this event he said, 'My photographs are, I think, unique, for no one seemed to think of anything but escape.' After escaping from the Turks again at Volo, he foolishly went back to recover 'two horses, my bicycle and a toothbrush' and ended up inexplicably captured by the Greeks. Thus established as a war correspondent of the heroic school, he set out for India where there was trouble on the North-West frontier. Here he met up with Melton Prior again, who was covering the campaign for the *Illustrated London News*.

The incident in the sketch occurred on 9 November soon after the Battle of Dargai, when the British were advancing into the Tirah Valley. The territory was rugged and 'a detachment of sixteen men went down a wrong nullah, lost the main party, and were instantly cut up'. The Northamptonshires, whose men had been lost, went out to find their dead comrades. Bull's picture shows them recovering the corpses on 'Dhoolies'. The Pathan tribesmen were adept at guerilla tactics, hiding in the rough country and surprising any foraging parties which became separated from the main force.

RENÉ BULL
'War correspondents in danger from the Afridis'
1897–8 TIRAH VALLEY EXPEDITION
Facsimile
Photomechanical half-tone engraving
Black and White, 25 December 1897, p. 793

As the British continued their advance into the Maidan Valley, Melton Prior and René Bull were unfortunate enough to be with a party of Sikhs who were surprised by the Afridis. They escaped and both wrote dramatic accounts of the action, with drawings, for their respective journals.

Bull writes: 'Prior and I went on a looting party with an escort of forty Sikhs.' Near a ruined village four of them, including the two correspondents, went forward to reconnoitre and were cut off from the main party by the tribesmen. 'We blazed away with our four revolvers, and so did they with rifles. Then when we thought the game was up the rattle of a volley behind us spoke of welcome aid at last. An Afridi or two leapt into the air and dropped stone dead; the rest vanished before our unexpected escort.' The march into Tirah continued to be perilous and Bull said that 'the safest way to sleep is to dig a grave in the ground and slumber there; tents are out of the question, as they make a splendid mark on a moonlit night'.

RENÉ BULL

'War correspondents on the road to Khartoum'

1896–8 RECONQUEST OF THE SUDAN
Facsimile
Photomechanical half-tone engraving
Black and White, 20 August 1898, p. 232

After the failure to rescue Gordon at Khartoum, all was quiet in the Sudan for eleven years. A new British plan for reconquest under Kitchener got under way in 1896. The army travelled up the Nile by boat and a number of correspondents shared a native 'gyassa', which was towed by a gun boat. Bull's sketch shows Bennet Burleigh of the *Daily Telegraph*, W. Maxwell of the *Standard* and H. Weldon of the *Morning Post* writing up their notes on the journey, with lots of bottles stowed away to fortify themselves. Burleigh was scornful about some of the sixteen 'so-called representatives of the press' who were to accompany the expedition. 'Some of them represented anything but journals or journalism, the name of the newspaper being used merely as a cover for notoriety and medal hunting.'

Eventually the expedition safely passed the Sixth Cataract and disembarked for the journey across the desert. Here Bull described conditions as being 'too terrible for words. One suffers not so much from the heat as from the awful storms which have been raging ever since our arrival. Continuous clouds of dust render it impossible to see four yards in front of one. The tents refuse to stand upright in the sand storms, and as these tempests regularly increase at night sleep is nearly impossible. Everything is buried at the moment under heaps of dust and sand; we weep muddy tears all day long, for the eyes suffer terribly under the ceaseless irritation. . . . If only we could get decent water the rest would not matter, but the railway is now finished and we shall soon be on the move.'

RENÉ BULL
'*Battle of Omdurman : charge of the 21st Lancers*'
1896–8 RECONQUEST OF THE SUDAN
Facsimile
Photomechanical half-tone engraving
Black and White, 24 September 1898, p. 389

The Dervishes, now led by the Mahdi's
successor, the Khalifa, waited for the British at
Omdurman outside Khartoum. Bull described
the battle as 'a desperate fight, as would be a
battle fought by desperate men. . . . One could see
the Dervish army plainly, and it looked fully
40,000 strong; we could hear their commands
being given.' The Dervishes moved forward and
the British, 'drawn up in fighting array', formed
a line 'at least two miles long. . . . A finer force it
would be impossible to imagine.' At dawn Bull
rode out with Bennet Burleigh towards the
cavalry scouts. 'We could distinctly hear the
enemy singing and beating their tom-toms.
There was no doubt about it; they were going to
give us battle this time.'

The British gunboats opened fire at 5.30 a.m.
and the Khalifa's army advanced. 'The air was
swishing with bullets. . . . One could see the
Dervishes run and drop like rabbits in heaps, the
maxims especially doing ghastly work.' As the
fire slackened Bull and Burleigh approached the
battlefield. 'As far as one could see lay dead and
dying. Some were sitting upright gazing with big
vacant eyes, as if they were not quite sure what
they were doing there; others trying to stop
bleeding from big gaping wounds; others had
not sufficient strength to brush the hundreds of
flies from their wounds.' A Dervish darted out
from under their horse's legs and rushed at
them, but was shot by an officer. They rode on
to Sigral Hill where they joined Kitchener's
party, and were able to watch the British cavalry
charge. One of the Dervishes could be seen
holding the Khalifa's black banner. 'The dead
lay around in heaps.' The 21st Lancers 'were
rushing a river bed full of enemy.' At last the
man holding the banner fell. The British rode on
into Khartoum and captured the Khalifa, at last
avenging Gordon (*Black and White*, 1 October
1898).

RENÉ BULL

'Cyclist Scouts crossing a drift at Frere'
1899–1902 BOER WAR
Facsimile
Photomechanical half-tone engraving
Black and White, 13 January 1900, p. 49

Bull was with Melton Prior again in the early days of the Boer War, but when Ladysmith was surrounded he managed to escape with Bennet Burleigh on one of the special trains sent out of the town with the wounded. He wrote, 'I am mighty glad I had the sense to get out of Ladysmith in time, or else for these six weeks you could have had no work from me. I don't know how the ★ or ★ are getting on without their regular correspondents' (*Black and White*, 6 January 1900).

Bull joined the Ladysmith relief column under General Buller, which set out from the advance base at Frere on 14 December 1899. Describing the cyclist scouts, Bull wrote, 'The bicycle has proved itself very serviceable during the present war. The rider is less conspicuous than he would be on a horse, though of course he has to risk punctures and gears going out of order.' He felt that not enough scouting had been done, particularly before the Battle of the Tugela. 'Our men, especially the Irish brigade, simply were walked into death's door, through lack of proper reconnaissance. Our scouts probably had done what they could, but there were not enough of them.' From Frere, Buller's force went to Chievely and Bull described how 'for miles and miles one could see nothing but huge strings of bullock-carts, artillery, cavalry and infantry. The dust and heat were choking. I really think it was hotter than any day we had in the Soudan.'

Correspondents had also sometimes used bicycles on campaign, and Frederic Villiers actually had one with him in the Sudan. A special machine had in fact been designed for reporters, although it is doubtful whether any of them dared to use it. The bicycle was described as being sturdy and 'calculated to stand the wear and tear of rough riding across country. Upon the handlebar is to be attached a typewriter, on which the operator will record all his impressions of the battle surging around him . . .' (*The Regiment*, 24 October 1896).

Cyclist scouts
crossing a drift.

René Bull
FRERE.

RENÉ BULL
'*Dead heroes of the Battle of Colenso*'
1899–1902 BOER WAR
Facsimile
Photomechanical half-tone engraving
Black and White, 27 January 1900, p. 129

The Battle of Colenso took place on 15 December 1899, when the Boers intercepted Buller's army marching to the relief of Ladysmith. In a despatch published in *Black and White* on 13 January, Bull described how the British infantry advancing on the village of Colenso were met with raking fire. 'They took as much cover as possible behind small rocks, advancing, as it were, in fits and starts. When within about five hundred yards we could see them begin to drop, and return the enemy's fire. One could compare the battlefield to nothing better than to a storm of hailstones beating on to a huge dusty plain.' The unsuspecting British had walked right into an ambush and their gunners were stranded. 'The wily Boers allowed them to unlimber before opening their disastrous fire. The men worked like heroes, and fought their guns against overwhelming odds to the last. Down they went one by one till round each gun there was a heap of dead and dying. Every single man was shot down at the guns' (*Black and White* 10 January 1900).

Bull's drawing shows No. 5 gun, 14th Battery Royal Field Artillery, where only two men were left unwounded – 'one laid the gun whilst the other ran backwards and forwards with the ammunition.' After a few moments 'these two men were shot down and the gun alone was left standing.' Frank Stewart's illustration for the *Illustrated London News*, showing the rescue operation for the guns, can be seen on page 136.

RENÉ BULL
'*The Battle of Spion Kop. Effect of a lyddite shell among the Boers*'
1899–1902 BOER WAR
Facsimile
Photomechanical half-tone engraving
Black and White 24 February 1900, p. 299.

The year 1899 ended with another disastrous battle between Buller's army and the Boers at Spion Kop, where the British took the hill but were ordered to withdraw at the end of the day, thus losing 1,773 men for no purpose. Bull's despatch, published on 24 February, was written hurriedly in pencil. He said, 'It was a tremendous battle which ended in a disaster. . . . When day broke a heavy mist hung over the hill, and it was impossible to see fifty yards ahead, but the guns on both sides were in action, firing more or less at random.' Regiment after regiment climbed the hill, but on reaching the summit were subjected to fierce enemy fire. Early in the afternoon the King's Royal Rifles and the Scottish Rifles were ordered to charge the hill from the east side. 'No intimation was sent to us

on the west, and we continued to shell the point, some of the shrapnel falling on our own men for an hour and a half.' The hill was captured about 4.30 p.m. and the approach roads were blocked with ambulances. 'The rest seems a nightmare. I cannot even now realise it can be true and that our troops are retiring. . . . It is impossible to tell you our feelings. I advanced to the Tugela, and there we met ambulance after ambulance, stretcher after stretcher on every side; graves were being dug, and gloom rested over the whole camp.' Ladysmith was not relieved until March.

René Bull's later career included some book illustrating – *La Fontaine's Fables* (1905), *The Arabian Nights* (1912) and *The Russian Ballet* (1913). He joined the RNVR in the First World War and later the RAF, and after the war worked for the Air Ministry. With the First World War the conventions of war reporting changed. Bull had started work at the end of the great period when the Henty-inspired reporter was the fashion, and might have found it difficult to adapt later to a more understated style.

Effect of a Lyddite Shell
among the Boers on the
north end of Spion Kop

René Bull 1900

159

RICHARD CATON WOODVILLE
(1856–1927)
'*All That was Left of Them*'
1899–1902 BOER WAR
Photomechanical half-tone engraving
Supplement to 'Holly Leaves' in the *Illustrated
Sporting and Dramatic News*
National Army Museum

It is Caton Woodville who is best remembered as
a war illustrator of the nineteenth century.
'There is scarcely a soldier, to say nothing of
civilians, whose pulse does not beat higher as he
looks on the realistic productions of Mr Caton
Woodville's wonderful brush' (Roy Compton,
The Idler, 1896). In fact, although an ex-captain
of the Royal North Devon Hussars, Caton
Woodville had seen little action. In 1876 he
completed some sketches at the front for the
Illustrated London News during the
Russo–Turkish War and was in Egypt in 1882,
arriving after most of the fighting was over. He
also went to the United States during the Sioux
uprising in 1891 where he met the American
artist Frederic Remington.

Caton Woodville's strength was to recreate
dramatic incidents from the British imperial wars

in a wholly imaginative way, without help from a
'special's' sketch. His knowledge of military
uniforms and incidental detail was exact. Apart
from his work as an illustrator, he painted huge
canvases with similar themes, some of which
went to Queen Victoria who was a great admirer
of his work.

This extraordinary picture is supposed to
illustrate an incident at Moddersfontein on 17
September 1901 when C Squadron of the
Lancers was surprised and surrounded by Boers.
All Caton Woodville's paintings show individual
acts of heroism, so that they have a moral and
universal meaning. They do not pretend to be
realistic but are always good propaganda,
representing British actions in the best possible
light. Frederic Villiers, who had some of the
same qualities, admired Caton Woodville's work,
saying that although he had 'never witnessed a
shot fired in anger nor seen anything of
campaigning, yet in his pictures there is all the
real dash and movement of war' (*Peaceful
Personalities and Warriors Bold*). A more critical
journalist writing in the 1880s said that
Woodville's illustrations were 'an artist's victory
over many a British defeat.'

C. E. FRIPP
Dec. 1894.

CHARLES EDWIN FRIPP (1854–1906)

'Chinese troops near Laichow on the way to Chefoo'

1894–5 SINO–JAPANESE WAR
Facsimile
Photomechanical half-tone engraving
Graphic, 2 March 1895, p. 237

Charles Fripp was the son of a landscape painter, George A. Fripp, and had studied art at the Royal Academy of Munich. He had an irascible personality and an independent turn of mind, which made him the subject of anecdotes among other correspondents. He had a long career as a 'special', first representing the *Graphic* at the Kaffir War of 1878 and the Zulu War of 1879. Here he was noticed by Archibald Forbes, who mentions 'a skilful artist of an independent nature, who, although wholly unaggressive when unmeddled with, had a will of his own.' He was fond of swimming, regardless of Zulus, and when ordered out of the river by an officer refused to budge, in spite of bullets, until he had finished his bathe. At last the exasperated officers removed him from danger by force (*Graphic*, 6 December 1890). On another occasion he had to be held down by Melton Prior to stop him

punching General Buller who had annoyed him.

He represented the *Graphic* in South Africa in 1881 and in the Sudan in 1885. He was with the Chinese forces at the Sino–Japanese War, while George Bigot was the *Graphic's* representative with the Japanese. This sketch was completed by Fripp in the winter of 1894. By this time the Japanese had taken Port Arthur and Wei-hai-wei, the fortresses guarding the entrance to the Gulf of Pechili. Laichow (Yehsien) and Chefoo (Yentai) were on the Shantung peninsula, which the Japanese were now attacking. The Chinese are dressed to withstand the cold. Fripp said that the Chinese soldiers were 'well accustomed to do with little, and with their bread and cabbage, and a little rice, can manage to get through a good deal of work.' However, 'in spite of their purchases of arms and ammunition and their borrowing of officers from Europe' their army had little improved 'since the days of bows and arrows and matchlock guns. Their soldiers are merely an armed rabble, brave enough when it comes to a hand-to-hand fight from which they cannot escape, but utterly uninterested in the war and without a particle of trust or belief in their leaders. Their hatred and loathing of the Japanese is intense.'

CHARLES EDWIN FRIPP
'The City's Own in action near Pretoria : how a detachment of the C.I.V. brought its Maxim into play at Diamond Hill'
1899–1902 BOER WAR
Original drawing
Pen and ink
National Army Museum

When the *Daily Graphic* commenced publication in 1890 Fripp's sketches appeared there as well as in the *Graphic*. On his return from China he was sent to America, travelling there by means of a package tour organized by the Klondike Mining, Trading and Transport Corporation, and between 1898 and 1899 he sent back lively reports and sketches of the American West. Towards the end of 1899 he was attached to the United States Army and covered the Philippines campaign during the Spanish–American War.

   This Boer War picture was reproduced in the *Daily Graphic* on 26 July 1900 and was drawn from notes provided by Captain Edis who had been present at the action. The British occupied Pretoria on 5 June 1900, and the sketch shows the C.I.V.s bringing their Maxim into use at Diamond Hill on 18 June. Fripp wrote, 'They brought their Maxim over the roughest ground – almost carrying it – and managed to keep it in action for about a quarter of an hour, to the great discomfort of the enemy, notwithstanding a cross fire of "pom poms" and field guns. As usual the Boers got into a nest of rocks, but in spite of the impregnable position which they held, the discretion of valour compelled them to retire with a couple of wagon loads of dead.'

CHARLES EDWIN FRIPP
'British soldiers searching a Boer Farm'
1899–1902 BOER WAR
Original drawing
Black, grey and white wash
National Army Museum

In spite of the British occupation of Pretoria, organized Boer resistance did not come to an end but continued spasmodically until 1902. There was a delay of about six weeks on Fripp's despatches before they were published in London. This sketch of British soldiers searching a Boer farm does not appear to have been published, although many other drawings done in the Pretoria region at this time appeared in the *Daily Graphic* between July and September 1899.

On 11 August the *Daily Graphic* reported how 'every farm was deserted by the men, who were away fighting, the women being left behind to appeal to the clemency of the General.' Boer farmsteads were often miniature arsenals with 'spare Mausers being buried or hidden beneath

the floor until the owner should return.' Sometimes British troops were fired on from farms when 'the white flag was flying as a symbol of neutrality', so it paid to search all buildings carefully for arms. Looting also sometimes occurred and the soldiers in Fripp's sketch seem to be taking an undue interest in the geese.

After the Boer War Fripp went to live in Canada, where he died at the age of fifty-two in 1906.

W. T. MAUD (1865–1903)

'*After the battle of Velestino : Greeks bringing their wounded down to the railway*'

1897 TURKO–GREEK WAR

Photomechanical half-tone engraving, redrawn by
G. P. Jacomb-Hood

Graphic, 22 May 1897, Supplement, p. 4

The *Daily Graphic*'s best war illustrator in the 1890s was W. T. Maud. The paper reproduced an artist's sketches in facsimile, and sometimes more elaborate versions were redrawn by staff artists for the *Graphic* – a much less satisfactory procedure. Maud had trained at the Royal Academy and before joining the *Daily Graphic* had worked as an illustrator and published some sketches in *Punch*. His first assignment as a 'special' was to cover the Armenian massacres in 1895. The following year he was sent to the rebel side in Cuba, and April 1897 saw him with the Greek army in Thessaly for the war against Turkey. W. K. Rose, the Reuter's

correspondent, first met Maud at Pharsala, and they were together until the Turkish victories drove the Greeks from Velestino. Rose later wrote, 'I had the pleasure of watching him, often under fire, making his powerful and picturesque sketches' (*With the Greeks in Thessaly*).

Maud described for the *Graphic* how 'the superior numbers and the superior generalship of the Turks have enabled them to turn, and thus render untenable, the Greek positions.' 'Smolenski, the commander of the Greek right wing, after making a fairly successful stand at Velestino, shared the fate of the main body and had to retire along the western shore of the Gulf of Volo to Armyro. And thus the entire Greek army found itself driven southwards until it was close to the old frontier line of 1831, having lost the richest province of Greece.' The Greeks were able to get this party of wounded on to the train and away from Velestino a few minutes before the Turks occupied the town.

W. T. MAUD

'For the coming siege : embarking the heavy guns for the storming of Omdurman at Atbara Camp'
1896–8 RECONQUEST OF THE SUDAN
Facsimile
Photomechanical line engraving
Daily Graphic, 29 August 1898, p. 4 bottom

Maud was next sent by the *Daily Graphic* to the Sudan and he was on the march to Abu Hamed in November 1897. He left the country at the end of the year for the North-West Frontier, returning in May 1898 in time to cover Kitchener's big push towards Omdurman.

Maud's sketch shows the heavy guns arriving in readiness for the advance. 'Strong fatigue parties of Egyptian troops are drawn up on either side of the line, and in an incredibly short space of time the guns are taken out of the train, hauled through the deep sand, and placed in position on the Nile bank, ready to be shipped on the Ghiassehs.' Watching two 40 pdr. guns being embarked, Maud wrote, 'These monstrous,

unwieldy-looking pieces of ordnance were easily moved about by the gunners with a rapidity which was simply astonishing.' Each gun weighed over five tons and had to be taken down the steep soft sand on to the river boat. This task was done in twenty minutes. 'These great siege guns looked strangely out of place in this desert camp, their wheels sunk almost to the axles in sand.' The guns would be taken to Omdurman by boat and then dragged on shore into position when the attack developed.

Sixteen members of the press were to accompany the advance. Kitchener would have preferred correspondents to stay at the base camp, but after the proprietor of *The Times* appealed to the Prime Minister, he was forced to allow them to go with him. Operations commenced in the middle of August and by the 27th Maud recorded that 'the health of the force is excellent. With the exception of an epidemic of enteric fever, in which the Lincolns lost most heavily, there has been practically no sickness, although some of the men caught chills through bathing in the river.'

W. T. MAUD

'On the way to Omdurman: how the Daily Graphic *sketches were sent down the Nile during the march to Wad Habesha*'
1896–8 RECONQUEST OF THE SUDAN
Facsimile
Photomechanical line engraving
Daily Graphic, 16 September 1898, p. 5 bottom

On 23 August, Maud wrote from Wad Habesha, about fifty miles from Omdurman, saying that the march from Atbara had taken seven days. Some of the men had been affected by sunstroke. 'A long march in the Soudan is a hugely monotonous performance, for there is little or nothing to distinguish one day from another.' Maud was with the party that went along the left bank of the river. The staff, the infantry, guns, stores and some more favoured correspondents went by boat.

Correspondents had their usual problem of getting despatches home. Maud described his solution: 'While on the march we sent down our telegraphs and letters by swimmers. There was never any difficulty in finding a native who was ready to embark on a sixty mile voyage down the river with only a log of wood as a support. . . . The postman hunted about along the river bank until he found a suitable log, launched it, wrapped his only garment in a huge coil round his head with the letters inside, and departed.' He was given six shillings at the start, and another six shillings on arrival. 'The Nile stream is running about five miles an hour, so our mail will travel quicker to Atbara Camp by water than by camel, which is the only other means of communication' (dated 23 August, ten days before the Battle of Omdurman).

Maud was present at the Battle of Omdurman and one of his sketches showing a Dervish charge formed the basis of a drawing in the *Graphic* on 24 September. His talent was not suited to grand subjects, and his quick sketches showing incidents in camp life or anecdotes of war are of far greater interest.

W. T. MAUD

'The Highlanders: the rifles get too hot to hold'

1896–8 RECONQUEST OF THE SUDAN
Facsimile
Photomechanical line engraving
Daily Graphic, 24 September 1898, p. 5 bottom

There were two Highland regiments at the Battle of Omdurman, the Camerons and the Seaforths. The Dervishes attacked at dawn and the artillery on both sides opened fire. As the battle progressed the Highlanders were singled out for attention by a party of Dervishes and in less than fifteen minutes twenty-five Camerons and twelve Seaforth Highlanders were casualties. Maud wrote, 'The Highlanders were firing very heavily, and their rifles became so heated in consequence that the men could not hold them. Colonel Money, however, was equal to the occasion, and ordered the men in reserve to bring up their cool rifles, which they handed to the men in the fighting line.'

After Omdurman Maud returned home and in December read a paper to the Society of Arts on 'Egypt and the Soudan in 1897 and 8'. He said that his first view of Omdurman was from the top of Kerreri Hill and he was 'among those who dismounted and scrambled to the top to look out upon the doomed city. From the hill top they could see the gunboats firing.'

W. T. MAUD

*'The Man of Straw: another little joke of the
5th Lancers at Observation Hill, Ladysmith'*
1899–1902 BOER WAR
Facsimile
Photomechanical line engraving
Daily Graphic, 4 January 1900, p. 8

On 29 September 1899 the *Daily Graphic*
reported that Maud had left for South Africa. He
was described as 'an undoubtedly clever artist,
with an eye for a good subject, and with the
ability to transfer that sketch rapidly to his
notebook; he is also a descriptive writer of no
mean order.' He was trapped in Ladysmith
during the siege, and shared a house there with
George Steevans of the *Daily Mail*. By
November the Boers were shelling the town day
and night. To keep their spirits up the defenders
published siege journals, *The Ladysmith
Bombshell*, and the *Ladysmith Lyre* edited by
Steevans. Maud described how a colleague tried
to photograph the falling shells: 'Whenever a
shell falls near the Mulberry Grove he rushes out
with his "Kodak" at full cock, and, in the

excitement of the moment he sends my little
table and papers flying.' He and Steevans had a
shelter in the garden, and he noticed that
'miraculous escapes from shells are getting so
common in Ladysmith that unless a man is
absolutely hit no one takes any notice'.

Maud sent some morale-boosting sketches
back to London of British attempts to distract
Boer gunners. On 29 December 1899 a sketch of
his called 'Playing with the Boers' appeared in
the *Daily Graphic*, showing a trooper holding up
a British helmet on a stick to draw the enemy's
fire. This sketch 'The Man of Straw' is a similar
dodge. 'The Lancers made a straw man, put a
soft felt hat on its head, and then elevated it with
a long pole. The result was instantaneous.
Hundreds of bullets riddled it through and
through, the soft felt hat was sent flying, and
down came the straw man, as though shot dead;
but he was passed a little further along the ridge,
the position of his arm was altered, and he
reappeared with the same successful result. The
game was kept up at intervals through the day,
and the Boers finally fired three shells at the man
of straw.'

W. T. MAUD
*'Some of White's heroes: the Manchesters
defending Caesar's Camp against the Boer
attack on January 6'*
1899–1902 BOER WAR
Facsimile
Photomechanical line engraving
Daily Graphic, 3 April 1900, p. 20 bottom left

Most of Maud's drawings did not reach the
Daily Graphic until after Ladysmith was
relieved, but he kept at work despite narrow
escapes from Boer shells. H. W. Nevinson,
correspondent of the *Daily Chronicle*, wrote on 2
December 1899, 'the narrowest escape was when
a great fragment flew through an open door and
cut the leg clean off a table where Mr Maud of
the *Graphic* sat at work' (*Ladysmith : Diary of a
Siege*).

Conditions in the town got worse towards
Christmas, and Maud's great friend Steevans
was among the many who died from enteric
fever. Nevinson said that 'for five weeks Maud
had nursed him with a devotion that no woman
could surpass', and that when Steevens had
realized his condition was hopeless the two of
them had drunk a last glass of champagne
together. After his friend's death Maud
volunteered to join the army, was given a
commission and made ADC to General Sir Ian
Hamilton. He assured the editor of the *Graphic*
that 'my military duties in no way interfered
with my work'. He saw some active service and
resigned his commission when Ladysmith was
relieved.

The incident in the sketch occurred when the
Boers made a final attempt to take the town on
6 January 1900, knowing that Buller's relief force
was almost there. During the Boer attack this
remote corner of Caesar's Camp was held by
sixteen men of the Manchester Regiment from
3.00 a.m. until dusk, when the Devonshires
reinforced them. 'Fourteen of the little band lay
dead, and of the two survivors one was wounded,
but they still held their position.' Maud had gone
up to the Camp by a cattle track to observe the
battle. 'Now and again, as I walked along,
Mauser bullets struck the ground with a scarcely
perceptible thud, and little puffs of dust rose
here and there above the grass.' The Boer attack
was repelled at the expense of heavy British
casualties.

Bulwana "Long Tom" firing.

W. T. MAUD

'*Cover for the "Cloth" : Archdeacon Barker
and his family taking shelter during the Siege
of Ladysmith*'
1899–1902 BOER WAR
Facsimile
Photomechanical line engraving
Daily Graphic, 29 March 1900, p. 5 bottom

A besieged poet wrote in the *Ladysmith Lyre* :

One thing is certain in this town of lies :
If Long Tom hits you on the head you dies.

The inhabitants of Ladysmith sought refuge in the
caves beside the Klip River when Long Tom and
the other siege guns were shelling the town. On 6
November 1899, H. W. Nevinson recorded in his
diary that 'the Archdeacon has hollowed out a
noble, ecclesiastical burrow' beside the river. On
12 November Nevinson described how the Boers
'conduct this siege with real consideration and
gentlemanly feeling.' They observed the
Sabbath, gave a day's rest after a violent
bombardment, and 'their hours of slaughter are
six to six, and they seldom overstep them. They
knock off for meals – unfashionably early, it is
true, but it would be petty to complain.'
This sketch was among the fifty Maud posted

to the *Daily Graphic* on 2 March after
Ladysmith was relieved. Describing it, Maud
said, 'The church and the vicarage were in one of
the most shell-swept parts of the town.
Archdeacon Barker had a shelter pit dug in the
river bank near his house, and whenever the
bombardment became very severe he took refuge
there with his family. The young ladies never
forgot to bring their pet birds with them.'
Maud watched the British troops riding into
the town, but he had caught enteric fever from
the dirty water tanks at Caesar's Camp and was
soon taken to hospital at Durban dangerously ill.
In a private letter, the last one he sent from
Ladysmith, he wrote, 'We have had a horrible
time of it – one I shall never forget as long as I
live. . . . What with deaths from shot, shell,
starvation and disease, we have but a shattered
remnant of the fine force that came up here last
October.' The *Graphic* paid tribute to 'his
indefatigability and conscientiousness – during
the siege he had duplicates of his huge budget of
sketches in order that those lost in the perilous
transit of siege time should not be irreplaceable.'
Although he worked again as a war
correspondent for the *Graphic*, his health never
really recovered and he died in Aden, in 1903, on
a homeward journey from Somaliland.

GEORGE LYNCH
'Mr Lynch's captivity : a rubber of whist with the enemy'
1899–1902 BOER WAR
Photomechanical half-tone engraving, redrawn by Allan Stewart
Illustrated London News, 10 February 1900, p. 185
bottom

George Lynch was a correspondent rather than an artist, and his sketch has been redrawn by Allan Stewart. He represented the *Morning Herald, Echo* and *Illustrated London News* at the Boer War, and became bored when shut up in Ladysmith, apparently for the duration of the siege. In search of copy he ventured out towards the Boer lines. W. T. Maud sent an account of his escapade to the *Daily Graphic* saying, 'A newspaper correspondent named Lynch, having asked the General's permission to go to the Boer lines to distribute copies of the *Ladysmith Lyre* was, of course, refused, so he bought a white umbrella, and rode in the direction of Pepworth Hill on a grey horse painted Kharki colour on one side only. He carried fifty copies of the paper

and a bottle of whisky – a sure recommendation to the Boers. He has not been seen since.'

The Boers when they caught him were understandably puzzled, but after deciding that he was not a spy, treated him well. His sketch shows him in a train with his captors. They were 'just in the middle of an interesting rubber, and passing through fields of luxuriant veldt some miles below Majuba, when a young Boer got into the carriage, and hearing from them in Dutch what I was, asked me – "What do you think of our new Transvaal, only two months old?". I had just time to say it looked wonderfully well considering its age, when Wicht snapped at him "Shut up! No politics please!"' Lynch suggested a race meeting or football match between the besiegers and besieged, but was soon put in his place by an elderly Boer who said: 'The only game we like to play now is the one with cannonballs' (George Lynch, *The Impressions of a War Correspondent*). Lynch felt that the Boers lacked the light touch of the British in their attitude to war: 'these dour, solid men take their fighting sadly and sternly.' After urgent representations from London, Lynch was released as a non-combatant.

ROBERT STEPHENSON SMYTH, LORD BADEN-POWELL (1857–1941)

'Familiarity breeds contempt : a race for a spent shell in besieged Mafeking'
1899–1902 BOER WAR
Photomechanical line engraving, redrawn by Reginald Cleaver
Daily Graphic, Siege of Mafeking Supplement, p. 9 top

Baden-Powell, who was in command at Mafeking during the siege, had for some years been sending sketches of military life to the *Daily Graphic*. His name was not written under his pictures from Mafeking for security reasons, but they were captioned 'from a sketch by a British officer, brought by runner to Bulawayo.' Baden-Powell had trained himself to see only the cheery side of war. A month before the relief of Mafeking he wrote, 'All blooming and booming here. We shan't know what to do with ourselves if we get relieved, we're so accustomed to our imprisonment now' (A. C. R. Carter, *Work of War Artists in South Africa*).

The story which this sketch illustrates was related by Baden-Powell in the *Daily Graphic* on 3 February 1900. 'The people are all so accustomed now to the shelling that they watch where each shell falls and run out to pick up the pieces. Sometimes a "blind" and spent shell comes along and there is great competition to capture it. One fell the other day between the women's camp and one of the forts, and there was an exciting race between the occupants of both positions to capture the shell while it was yet bounding and tumbling along the ground, although to have touched it before it stopped would probably have meant at least a broken bone.' This rather unbelievable incident might be partly explained by an entry in Sol T. Plaatje's Diary for 18 January 1900: 'The Boers are using some marvellous shells just now. . . . They seldom burst where they first land, but merely plough the ground for a little distance, then pump right up in the air again and start a fresh journey for one or two more miles before they reach their fag end.' In fairness to Baden-Powell, the facetious approach was encouraged by the *Daily Graphic* and its other main war artists of the period, W. T. Maud and C. E. Fripp, also sometimes caricatured their subjects.

GEOFFREY DOUGLAS GILES (1857–?)
*'With French in Cape Colony : scenes in camp
at Naauwpoort'*
1899–1902 BOER WAR
Original drawing
Pen and ink
National Army Museum

G. D. Giles was another of the *Graphic*'s
representatives at the Boer War, and travelled
with the Kimberley Relief Column. He was an
experienced painter of military and hunting
scenes and exhibited at the Royal Academy in
1884 and 1888, and at the Salon de Paris in 1885.
He had served in the Indian Army, retiring as a
Major in 1884. General French commanded the
cavalry division of the Kimberley Relief
Column, and the incident in the sketch probably
occurred in December 1899 when French was in
Cape Colony at Naauwpoort on the Port
Elizabeth Railway. The *Graphic* of 13 January
1900 described how he had been doing good
work 'fighting the Boers at their own game' from
his base at the railway junction at Naauwpoort.
From here he advanced to Arundel and
Rensburg, and on New Year's Day 1900
occupied the heights overlooking the west of

Colesberg. The British objective was to stop the
invasion of Cape Colony by Free State Boers,
drive the enemy across the Orange River and
then march on Bloemfontein. French is on the
right of Giles's sketch supervising the cavalry
who are getting ready for the advance.

CHARLES M. SHELDON (1866–?)
'*Interior of the Stone Fort at El Caney after the bombardment*', *1 July 1898*
1898 SPANISH–AMERICAN WAR
Facsimile
Photomechanical line engraving
Black and White, 27 August 1898, p. 263 bottom

Charles Sheldon was born in Indiana in 1866 and first worked for his father who was a publisher. In his twenties he travelled through the Southern States of America as special correspondent of the American Press Association and later ran an engraving business in Kansas. In 1890 he came to Paris where he worked under Lefèvre and Constant, and during this time sent sketches of Parisian events to *Pall Mall Budget*. Later he worked regularly for *Black and White* and for *The Ludgate Magazine* in London. He was a war correspondent in the Sudan in 1896, in Cuba during the Spanish–American War and went on to South Africa in 1899 to cover the Boer War. His sketch of the interior of El Viso fort at El Caney was published simultaneously in

Leslie's Weekly in America and *Black and White* in England. He wrote in *Leslie's :* 'It was simply punched to pieces. . . . The walls were between two and three feet thick, and inside the fort were whitewashed sheds for the protection of the soldiers against the weather. The garrison was practically all killed, and lay about among the debris of splintered and tumbled walls. Nearly all of them were wounded, not once, but many times. Looking down on the position from which we attacked, the wonder simply is that we were not absolutely annihilated.'

FREDERIC REMINGTON (1861–1909)
'*The opening of the fight at Wounded Knee*'
1867–91 INDIAN WARS
Facsimile
Photomechanical half-tone engraving
Harper's Weekly, 24 January 1891, p. 65

Frederic Remington's illustrations begin to appear in *Harper's Weekly* in 1882. Remington was born in New York in 1861 and first went to Montana in the West in 1881 when he was nineteen. In 1883 he went to live on a Kansas ranch for a year, and between 1886 and 1889 more than a hundred Remington illustrations of Western life were published in *Harper's*.

Remington was one of the many illustrators who recorded the Indian troubles of 1890–1891, which culminated in the massacre of the Sioux at Wounded Knee. He met Caton Woodville of the *Illustrated London News* on this campaign and found that they had much in common. Both loved the drama and excitement of outdoor life in the West, and both were inclined to leave out of their drawings the worst horrors of war.

Remington described for *Harper's* how he rode into Pine Ridge Agency 'very hungry and nearly frozen to death' and met officers of the 7th US Cavalry who had been in the fighting. 'They told me their stories in that inimitable way which is studied art with warriors. Lieutenant Mann said: "I saw three or four young bucks drop their blankets, and I saw that they were armed." An Indian medicine man then threw dust in the air, which was a sign of war, and "those bucks stripped and went into action". The Indians believed that "the white men's bullets would not go through the ghost shirts".' At least 300 of the Sioux died in the fight. One of the Indian women, Louise Weasel Bear said, 'they shot us like we were buffalo. I know there are some good white people, but the soldiers must be mean to shoot children and women' (Dee Brown, *Bury My Heart at Wounded Knee*).

FREDERIC REMINGTON

'Geronimo and his band returning from a raid into Mexico'

1867–91 INDIAN WARS

Wood engraving

Harper's Weekly, 18 August 1888, p. 609

After the completion of the railway to the Pacific, artists and reporters from all countries made their way to the West, and pictures showing the life there figure prominently in the illustrated papers of the last part of the nineteenth century. The Civil War artists Al Waud, Theodore Davis and Alfred Matthews, in need of work once the war was over, were among the first to go. British journals also sent their 'specials' and these included all the famous names – William Simpson, Sydney Hall, Melton Prior, Frederic Villiers, Richard Caton Woodville and Charlie Fripp.

This illustration by Frederic Remington shows the Apache chief Geronimo who was alleged to have left the reservation and gone on the war path because he had been imposed upon and robbed by white people, and accused of crimes which had been committed by Mexicans. Remington did not altogether believe this and went on to say, 'The facts are that Geronimo made his first overtures of surrender only when he had been fairly run down by Captain Henry Lawton's troop of 4th Cavalry.' After a chase through the mountains they overtook him on the banks of the Bavispe River in Sonora. The Apaches had no alternative but to surrender. 'It was a picturesque sight when this savage horde came over the mountain pass leading down to San Bernardino, riding at full speed, and driving the stolen horses and cattle before them.'

FREDERIC REMINGTON

'The charge of the Rough Riders at San Juan Hill', 1 July 1898

1898 SPANISH–AMERICAN WAR

Oil painting

Remington Art Museum

When Remington went to Cuba as war 'special' for *Harper's Weekly* he expressed the opinion, 'I am, so far as I know, the only accredited correspondent on this expedition, and yet there are on this ship alone six enlisted privates who correspond regularly with the newspapers at home.' He felt that these men 'are bound to use the press to criticize their officers.' When he landed at Siboney he joined up with the regular press corps, and watched the shelling of El Caney. The charge of the Rough Riders at San Juan Hill was a subject which he later came back to again and again in paintings and drawings.

This oil painting was completed from sketches made at the time and shows the 1st US

Volunteer Cavalry who 'formed the most picturesque regiment in the army', although they were looked upon by regulars as 'cow-punchers and college boys' (Richard Harding Davis, *Cuba in War Time*). It was necessary for the American troops to take the San Juan fort in order to open the way to Santiago. Theodore Roosevelt led the Rough Riders in a charge. Richard Harding Davis described how they 'worked their way to the front, broke through a skirmish-line of regulars, and with Roosevelt leading them on horseback, took a fortified casa to the right – Roosevelt killing a Spaniard with his pistol. . . . A little later we crossed the trenches and went into the captured fort of San Juan. It was little more than a well-fortified blockhouse, and I counted but seven dead Spaniards about.' Remington had some narrow escapes in the action. As the bullets flew past him, 'I dropped in the tall guinea-grass, and crawled to some soldiers, hidden under a mango tree. I think that episode cost me my sketch book.'

FREDERIC REMINGTON
'Field hospital at the "Bloody Ford" of San Juan Creek'
1898 SPANISH–AMERICAN WAR
Facsimile
Photomechanical half-tone engraving
Harper's Weekly, 24 December 1898, p. 1268–9

Theodore Roosevelt, describing the battle afterwards in *The Rough Riders*, wrote: 'The Mauser bullets drove in sheets through the trees and the tall jungle grass, making a peculiar whirring or rustling sound. . . . After the battle of San Juan my men had really become veterans.' A field hospital was established beside a creek near the battle area. Dr Newgarden, Regimental Surgeon of the 3rd US Cavalry, has left this description: 'There was a cut bank, varying from a few inches to about three feet high, serving as partial protection for a man lying down behind it, and in some places for one even sitting.' Boughs and leaves were gathered together to make beds, and the hospital was hardly ready before the firing started. 'The first thing that impressed me was the curious expression of the faces of the wounded. None were without it, except those mortally hurt. As nearly as I can interpret it into words, the look was one of "dazed anxious surprise". . . . Now and then a wounded horse would plunge through the station.'

HOWARD CHANDLER CHRISTY
(1873–1952)
*'Second Infantry landing at Siboney', 24 June
1898*
1898 SPANISH–AMERICAN WAR
Facsimile
Photomechanical half-tone engraving
Leslie's Weekly, August 1898

Howard Chandler Christy made his reputation as
an illustrator representing *Leslie's Weekly* at the
Spanish–American War. With other
correspondents he watched the American troops
land in Cuba on 22 June 1898. Richard Harding
Davis described how 'under the cover of the
smoke the long-boats and launches began to
scurry toward the shore. . . . A launch turned
suddenly and steered for a long pier under the
ore-docks, the waves lifted it to the level of the
pier, and half-a-dozen men leaped through the
air and landed on the pier-head, waving their
muskets above them' (*The Cuban and Porto
Rican Campaign*).

Davis was indignant that General Shafter had

not allowed the correspondents to land with the
first troops. The landings continued for three
days at Siboney and at Daiquiri further along the
coast. On the evening of 24 June more landings
were made on Siboney beach, and these are
shown in Christy's illustration. Two warships
flood-lit the beach 'and made Siboney as light as
a ball-room'. On the shore 'a thousand or so
naked men were assisting and impeding the
progress shoreward of their comrades, in
pontoons and shore-boats, which were being
hurled at the beach like sleds down a water-
chute.' The men were singing and 'dancing
naked around the camp-fires on the beach, or
shouting with delight as they plunged into the
first bath that had offered in seven days.' Away
from the shore some of the troops were drying
themselves beside the camp fires and the Rough
Riders, who had just marched in from Daiquiri,
were cooking bacon and coffee.

HOWARD CHANDLER CHRISTY

'Wounded Rough Riders walking into Siboney; Second Infantry marching to their relief'

1898 SPANISH–AMERICAN WAR
Facsimile
Photomechanical half-tone engraving
Leslie's Weekly 1 September 1898

The first land battle of the war was at Las Guasimas on 24 June 1898. General Young's brigade of the 1st and 10th Regular Cavalry advanced towards the Spanish along one path and Colonel Wood's 1st Volunteer Cavalry on another. Most of the correspondents went with the Rough Riders, and Christy has sketched their wounded returning to camp.

Richard Harding Davis attributed the American victory at Las Guasimas to the final charge of the Rough Riders. 'The Spaniards naturally could not believe that this thin line which suddenly broke out of the bushes and from behind the trees and came cheering out into the hot sunlight in full view, was the entire fighting force against it.' By the end of the day

the Americans had control of the entire Spanish position, but casualties were severe. One correspondent, who lost a leg in the battle, wrote, 'I saw many men shot. Every one went down in a lump without cries, without jumping in the air, without throwing up hands. They just went down like clods in the grass' (Edward Marshall, quoted in Frank Freidel's *The Splendid Little War*).

Christy's war pictures and articles appeared in *Leslie's* and *Harper's* and he helped to illustrate Wright's history of the war. He continued as a magazine illustrator after the war and also became known as a poster artist. In later years he devoted his time to portraiture.

ERNEST PRATER
'The Volunteer Ambulance at Work'
1899–1902 BOER WAR
Photomechanical line engraving, redrawn by
A. S. Hartrick
Sphere, 3 March 1900, Supplement, p. iv

Although the *Sphere* often published war drawings which had the appearance of being completed on the spot, the journal almost always had the 'special's' sketches redrawn for publication. Ernest Prater was a Londoner of Cornish descent who took up drawing after being in commerce for some years. He served for a period with the 3rd Middlesex Artillery, and specialized in military subjects in the London office when not on campaign. It is difficult to determine his skill as an artist as all his Boer War sketches were redrawn, although the *Sphere* did say that his pictures were of 'exceptional merit and would delight the eye of the most exigent

master of an art class by their conscientious draughtsmanship.'

Prater was with General Buller's troops and the incident in the sketch occurred after the battle of Spion Kop in January 1900, when the British suffered heavy casualties. Winston Churchill described for the *Morning Post* how 'a village of ambulance waggons grew up at the foot of the mountain. The dead and injured, smashed and broken by the shells, littered the summit till it was a bloody, reeking shambles. . . . Men were staggering along alone, or supported by comrades, or crawling on hands and knees, or carried on stretchers. Corpses lay here and there. Many of the wounds were of a horrible nature. The splinters and fragments of the shell had torn and mutilated in the most ghastly manner.' Prater noted that the ambulance bearers were 'typical colonists in appearance', and were men 'thrown out of employment by the war'.

ERNEST PRATER
'The Burial of the Dead at Vaal Krantz'
1899–1902 BOER WAR

Photomechanical line engraving, redrawn by Ralph
Cleaver
Sphere, 24 March 1900, p. 285

Many of Prater's sketches for the *Sphere* were
more concerned with propaganda than with an
accurate presentation of fact, as for example a
picture which appeared on 3 March 1900
showing the Boers robbing British dead and
wounded. Photographs were now used
extensively by the journal and sketches played a
subsidiary role. 'The photographer has now
become a far more potent personality in
illustrated journalism than hitherto, and all
special representatives of the *Sphere* carry the
camera as well as the sketch book' (27 January
1900).

Prater's account of this incident describes how
he rode out to Vaal Krantz the day after its
capture on 6 February 1900. 'On my way I met a
party of the Volunteer Ambulance who had been
collecting the dead and were in the act of burying
them in a grave by the side of the Tugela. It was
very impressive to see a private of the Durhams
who had come from the kopje take a prayer book
from his trouser pocket and read the burial
service over his dead comrades. I was told that
all had now been buried, but on proceeding
across the mealie patch I came across the body of
another Durham on his back in a donga. He had
been severely hit by a fragment of shell in the
head. I first found his helmet, a little further on
his rifle, and then his body. He had evidently
managed to stagger to the shelter of the donga
and lay down to die.'

Like so many other correspondents, Prater
succumbed to enteric fever some months later in
South Africa.

INGLIS SHELDON-WILLIAMS
(1870–1940)
'Japanese officer riding an ox and led by a soldier entering Pingyang'
1904–5 RUSSO–JAPANESE WAR
Facsimile
Photomechanical line engraving
Sphere, 4 June 1904, p. 219 top left

Photographs of the Russo–Japanese War published in the *Sphere* were particularly fine, and the drawings did not have the same authority. There had been a sharp decline in quality since the heyday of the artist in the 1880s and 1890s, and this was true for all the illustrated papers, although Prior and Villiers were still at work. Fashions had changed and photography was now the novelty. Paintings, which could be reproduced by the new half-tone process, were often used rather than line sketches and were cleverly printed to look as much like a photograph as possible. Inglis Sheldon-Williams's picture is one of the rare examples reproduced in facsimile from an original sketch. Sheldon-Williams had emigrated to Canada with his family at the age of sixteen and worked as an illustrator there. He represented the *Sphere* at

the Boer War and the Russo–Japanese War.

Japan had decisively beaten China in a dispute over Korea in 1895 but soon found that Russia had designs on the territory. Ping Yang was the most important town in North Korea, 150 miles north of Seoul, and had been fought over in the war with China. Having blockaded the Russian fleet in Port Arthur, the Japanese landed in Korea in May 1904 and advanced towards Ping Yang and the River Yalu, which formed the boundary between Manchuria and Korea.

The *Sphere* gave good coverage to the war, and had a special arrangement with *Collier's Weekly* of America so that both journals could publish each other's pictures and despatches. On 13 February 1904 the *Sphere* proudly stated, 'The *Sphere* will give only Illustrations from Sketches or Photographs from the Actual Scene of Operations. It will publish no Imaginary Drawings.' But this principle was loosely interpreted, and the majority of pictures were redrawn 'from a sketch' by the special artist.

Sheldon-Williams continued to work as an illustrator after the war, and during the First World War was official war artist to the Canadian Expeditionary Force.

ANON
The Union Jack

The Union Jack, Vol. I, No. 5, 29 January 1880.
Frontispiece

During the last quarter of the nineteenth century, British pride in imperial achievement was reflected in literature, painting and popular culture. The young were taught to believe implicitly in the ideal of Empire through the medium of popular adventure stories and comics, and those who grew up at the turn of the century never completely lost this way of thought. Rider Haggard and G. A. Henty were the leading writers for boys on imperial themes, and Henty, who had been a war correspondent, was the author of 'Times of Peril', here illustrated, which appeared in *The Union Jack*, 'Tales for British Boys'. The teenage heroes of this story had incredible adventures during the Indian Mutiny. Henty believed in the divine mission of the British to civilize and govern, and the native soldiers in the picture are being unceremoniously put to flight by unarmed British troops. The romantic image of imperial warfare, first fostered by the war correspondents, carried on to the twentieth century in the comics and books read by the younger generation, who never entirely lost their ideals until the horrors of the First World War and a greater realism in reporting and photography gradually made for a change of heart.

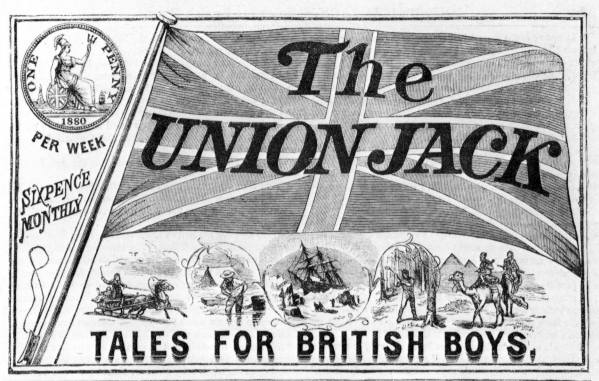

The UNION JACK

ONE PENNY
PER WEEK
1880

SIXPENCE MONTHLY

TALES FOR BRITISH BOYS.

Vol. I.—No. 5.]　　Edited by W. H. G. KINGSTON.　　[Jan. 29, 1880.
[All rights reserved.]

"WE BURST THROUGH THEM." (See p. 66.)

TIMES OF PERIL. A Tale of India.

By G. A. HENTY. (Continued from p. 53.)

CHAPTER V.

"How far is it to Delhi? We heard the guns there just now."

"Not thirty miles."

Index

Page numbers in italics refer to illustrations, usually accompanied by text on the same page.

CAMBRIA COUNTY LIBRARY
JOHNSTOWN, PA. 15901

CAMBRIA COUNTY LIBRARY   MN
Hodgson, Pat.

WITHDRAWN
Cambria Co. Library

8 5131

02